callas ^{by} callas

callas _{by} callas

Renzo & Roberto
ALLEGRI

callas by callas

The Secret Writings of "la Maria"

UNIVERSE

First published in the United States of America in 1998
by UNIVERSE PUBLISHING
A Division of Rizzoli International Publications, Inc.
300 Park Avenue South
New York, NY 10010

Front cover photograph: Archivio Editoriale Gli Olmi, Milan
Back cover photograph: Centro Documentazione Mondadori, Segrate

98 99 00 01 / 10 9 8 7 6 5 4 3 2 1

ISBN: 0-7893-0135-0

4

Printed and bound in Spain

Library of Congress Catalog Card Number: 98-14769

Editorial coordination
Franca Cambié

Art Director
Giorgio Seppi

Graphics layout
Marco Fogliatti

Editorial production
Il Faggio, Milan

English translation:
Peter Eustace, Verona

© 1997 Arnoldo Mondadori Editore S.p.A.,
Printed in Spain by
Artes Graficas Toledo, S.A.
D.L. TO: 82-1998

Contents

Preface

Thousands of articles and dozens of books have been published about Maria Callas. When she was alive, Callas always complained about what was written on her account, insisting it did not reflect the truth.

She attacked the press bitterly. If she could express her opinion of what has been published about her since her death, she would probably be even more indignant. So, why publish yet another book? Because we are sure that we have put together something truly different. This book, based on a collection of photographs dear to Callas herself (many of which have revealing comments in her own handwriting on the back), is not a biography in the conventional sense of the term; our intention, rather, is to weave together something as close to an autobiography as possible. We have culled the information from Callas herself, in the form of her various writings which reveal much about her life and its vicissitudes.

Someone once wrote that Callas was a lazy correspondent, never taking up pen and paper to reply to friend's letters. This is entirely untrue—Callas wrote a great deal. When she was in love, she was even prolific in letter-writing. Far away from her loved one, she wrote two, even three letters a day—letters of four, five, six pages, extraordinarily passionate and spontaneous. If everything Callas ever wrote were to be collected, it would make a fascinating book.

Most of her letters date from the years spent with her husband, Giovan Battista Meneghini. Our archives of this period contain hundreds of sheets of paper and notes. They are mostly love letters, which nevertheless provide much precious biographical information. Yet we also have the lengthy denials sent to newspapers, the memoranda for lawyers, and the meticulously detailed reconstructions of the scandalous episodes published in the gossip columns. Callas never complained when the press criticized her interpretations, even when the critics were unjustly harsh; but, she became furious when the stories were inaccurate, and battled determinedly to publish the truth.

Other important biographical details are to be found in the letters to her godfather, Dr. Leonidas Lantzounis, published in part by Arianna Stassinopoulos in her major biography of Callas. Other insights into Callas are revealed in her letters to her friend, John Ardoin, which he collected in another important book. The famous tenor Giuseppe Di Stefano owns some letters from Callas, penned during the time when they lived together. Although Di Stefano does not want them to be published, the letters were nevertheless briefly shown to us. The mysterious diary that Maria kept in the last two years of her life—also unpublished and owned by an Italian physician, Dr. Ivano Signorini (who equally wishes to keep its contents undisclosed)—was also shown to us, at least in part. There is also the great deal of material which Maria left about her own life. Almost all of this is unknown to those who have written and continue to write about her. Yet we feel that this information is essential if we are to understand Callas's soul and the secrets of her art. This is why our book is based largely on what we can only summarize in the title: Callas by Callas.

Renzo and Roberto Allegri

Four Greats Talk About Callas

CARLO MARIA GIULINI
Conductor

"Maria Callas was a very great artist. She was a perfect musician, with an extraordinary voice, and she perfected a technique which enabled her to exploit it to the fullest extent. Moreover, she was able to inhabit the role completely. These natural gifts were joined by her passion for singing, her determination to succeed, and her desire for perfection. When I worked with her, she was always the first to arrive at rehearsals and the last to leave. For the famous *Traviata* at La Scala in 1955, we worked on certain scenes for days on end, from morning to night. Her natural gifts and her immense commitment made her the superlative artist who is still much admired today.

"As a woman, on the other hand, she always remained an enigma to me. I was never able to determine who she really was. She became the role she was interpreting at any given moment. She transformed into the character and lived the experience intensely. Yet I always had the impression that when she wasn't a character on-stage, she was somewhat lost, disoriented. I have the feeling that she was possibly uncomfortable with herself."

FRANCO ZEFFIRELLI
Director

"When people become legends, they also become victims of the popular imagination, and it is impossible to distinguish between reality and fantasy. The image of Maria Callas which is generally portrayed has little to do with the true identity of the singer. The only thing that reflects reality concerns her art. This cannot be manipulated: There are recordings which make it perfectly clear that she was a great singer. And, as a singer, Maria is a well-documented myth.

"I think myself lucky that I was able to work with her but, especially, for having become a friend. When I met her, she was at the outset of her career. She was sturdy, even overweight. Everything about her was big: her eyes, her nose, her mouth. She later became very beautiful and very elegant. We directors taught her nothing. Our task was simply to clarify the wonderful intuitions which she had for every stage situation. Or to suggest ideas which she immediately and avidly took up with exceptional assimilative ability. It seemed as if there were two personalities inside her: One was an ordinary woman, simple, calm, the other a great artist.

I often watched her as she chatted backstage; she seemed more like an extra.

Her conversation was silly, superficial even. But as soon as she stood up to go onstage, a flash of lightning appeared in her eyes and she became pervaded with a potent energy: Maria became a goddess, an angel, a demon, a higher being, perfect, capable of dominating everything with her determination and her art."

BIKI
Fashion designer

"I met Maria Callas in the winter of 1951 at a dinner at the home of Arturo Toscanini. When I saw her arrive, accompanied by her husband Giovan Battista Meneghini, I was dumbfounded. I had never seen such a badly dressed woman. She was also very overweight, almost matronly. She knew nothing of elegance. At the dinner, she turned up wearing an enormous velvet hat, a pair of earrings with plastic clips and, as if that were not enough, a pair of black patent leather shoes. Nobody had ever told her that a lady should not wear a large hat after 5:00 P.M., and that such shoes ought to be abolished. When I saw her that evening I never dreamed that one day I would have designed her clothes.

"I saw her again three years later and she had transformed into a swan. The fat, ordinary figure had disappeared. Instead, the women who stood before me was beautiful and very elegant. I began to design clothes for her, but I never forced my hand, because Callas had taste and was attracted to everything beautiful. She was a perfectionist: She person-

ally selected the fabrics for her outfits. She sometimes even made suggestions. She had a weak point: her ankles. They were terribly large and she was very self-conscious of them. However, her face was unique, her comportment regal, and her hands were so slim that I often was sorry to make her wear gloves."

GIULIETTA SIMIONATO
Mezzo-soprano

"Maria: a sweet name, and Callas certainly knew how to be sweet. I got to know her possibly better than anyone else ever did. As she once defined me in the dedication on a photograph, I was her only friend in the music world. I don't exaggerate when I say that she was such a professional she never once missed a rehearsal or arrived late. She was humble and good. She was the personification of music, so much so that in Pasolini's film *Medea*, she was not at all herself without Cherubini. When I told her she thanked me. I could tell her everything, make fun of her, even tell her off. It was only when she died that I realized how close we had been."

9

Origins

A furious snowstorm engulfed New York on December 4, 1923, the day Maria Callas was born. An emblematic atmosphere for the beginning of a life which was destined to leave an indelible mark on the history of music.

"It's a strong, healthy girl—she weighs more than thirteen pounds!" exclaimed the doctor supervising the birth when passing a new daughter to Evangelia Dimitriadis, a Greek immigrant who had arrived in the United States only four months beforehand. Instead of smiling happily, the woman turned away her head and said: "I don't want to see her."

A sad and equally emblematic welcome. The girl destined to become the greatest opera singer of the century—

# of a Myth

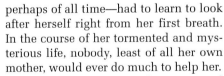

perhaps of all time—had to learn to look after herself right from her first breath. In the course of her tormented and mysterious life, nobody, least of all her own mother, would ever do much to help her.

Seventy-five years have passed since that day. In 1997, the world of music celebrated the fiftieth anniversary of Callas's official debut in a major opera theater, the Verona Arena, a debut which set her on her career. The year also commemorated the twentieth anniversary of the death of the singer.

It is almost impossible to find, in the world of opera, personalities who have been as adored as Callas. There are certainly singers who, on an artistic level, are by no means her inferior: Maria Malibran, for example, Enrico Caruso,

Beniamino Gigli. But these great artists never enjoyed the kind of vast popularity achieved by Callas.

And this popularity is still growing. Maria Callas is a unique example of a singer whose interpretations are never dated. Listening to them, no one can say, "That was how they sang in the fifties." This is because her renderings are alive, modern, and still avant garde. They are the expression of a unique, complex, and unpredictable personality—a personality which the trials of life imbued with drama and even tragedy. Whoever came close to Callas and had the fortune of penetrating her human and artistic mystery remained dazzled and unable ever to forget the experience.

But what are the roots of this myth? How did this artist, this extraordinary woman, develop? Where did she come from? What was her cultural background?

Generally speaking, the narratives in biographies of the "greats" are falsified by the reflection of their fame. The events in the years prior to glory are

reconstructed, and usually with an eye to future success. These descriptions tend to lose their genuineness, and cannot always be trusted.

In the case of Maria Callas, this "cliff" is steeper than ever. This is especially true because the people who witnessed her early years—her mother, sister, companions at the conservatory, her first colleagues—hardly ever told the truth when interviewed at the height of Maria's fame.

From our investigations into the most reliable documents, Maria's own writings in particular, it appears that her origins and early background have nothing to do with what happened later. Maria did not come from a family of intellectuals. Recollections of Greek culture were perhaps present only in her chromosomes; she grew up in a popular New York suburb, a seemingly flat and anonymous environment.

But she had the soul of a queen. This is the mysterious, inexplicable side. Callas never let herself be dominated by the consequences of poverty, nor

by the squalor of everyday life. She kept her dreams wholly intact, demonstrating a rich, prodigious, interior greatness.

Maria Callas is a paradigm of an artist who grew on her own, almost against her own will. It was as if she were guided by an enigmatic destiny. She confessed as much one day in 1970 to writer Dacia Maraini, with whom she had travelled in Africa in the company of Pier Paolo Pasolini and Alberto Moravia: "I feel privileged to have had a destiny other than the ordinary. I am a creature of destiny. Destiny took me, wanted me this way. I am outside myself and witness my own life from

the outside. I see myself clearly, I see other people."

Maria did not come from a family of musical geniuses, she did not receive strict cultural education, she was never the pupil of famous teachers, nor did she attend prestigious academies. She was born with the gifts that made her great. Not famous, as we are wont to say. The famous often end up as nullities.

Callas followed her instincts, guided by destiny, achieving heights which only after her death emerged in all their artistic importance. During her life, she was a difficult singer, controversial, often highly criticized. Today, Maria is a myth, a legend, and it seems impossible that anyone could not have admired her while she was alive. Today, millions of people would be well-disposed to travel great distances and spend enormous sums of money to see one of her concerts. Yet, new generations and new admirers of Callas should know that, when she was alive, she was not under-

stood by everyone and did not receive all the adulation she deserved.

Regarding Callas, music critics fell into two camps: The young were on her side, the older against her. The first of the younger critics to sense the artistic greatness of the Greek singer was Giuseppe Pugliese, then one of the leading musicologists of the up-and-coming generation and music critic for the Venice newspaper *Gazzettino*. Having heard her sing at the Fenice in the role of Isotta, he wrote: "An artist of uncommon musical sensitivity and captivating, sure stage presence, Maria Callas lived the amorous passion of her role more

with the transport of feminine sweetness than druidic virility. Yet her beautiful, warm voice expressed, especially in the high notes, shrill accents and a highly appropriate lyricism." Two months

and especially in terms of psychological vigor, singular expressive strength, and enchanting statuary, dramatic beauty. It has been a long time since I heard such a gifted and effective singer."

But not all the famous critics of the time thought in the same way. Callas's interpretive innovations, revolutionary for her time, shocked them. Her voice—extremely particular with a new and unusual timbre—perplexed them. Guido

"I saw the light in New York, born under the sign of Sagittarius, on the morning of December 2nd or 4th. I can't be sure about this, as for many of the circumstances of my life, since my passport declares I was born on the 2nd while my mother maintains I came into the world on the 4th."

later, listening to her in *Turandot* in Udine, he wrote again: "Callas was an exceptional Turandot. Her incomparable, clear, warm voice, powerful in all registers, carved out the difficult Oriental character most admirably, even

Pannain was the "prince" of Italian music critics in the 1950s. A composer, professor at Naples Conservatory, author of numerous books such as the celebrated *History of Music* in three volumes (in cooperation with Andrea Della Corte),

Opposite page, left:

1934. Maria Callas (in the foreground), aged eleven, with friends at Inwood Park, New York. She was born on December 4, 1923, at Flower Hospital, New York, the second child of a Greek family who had emigrated to America a few months earlier. She spent her infancy in Astoria, a Long Island suburb, where there was a large Greek community.

Opposite page, right:

1936. Maria Callas with her father, George, a pharmacist. Born in Greece in 1888, his real name was George Kalogeropoulos, a surname he changed to Callas upon emigrating to the United States. He died in Athens in 1972.

Left:

1937. Maria (first right) in New York with her father, George, mother Evangelia Dimitriadis (1889-1980?), and sister, Giacinta—known as Jackie—who was born in Greece in 1917. The Kalogeropoulos family also had a son, Vasily, born in 1920, who died the following year during the typhus epidemic.

Right:

1934. Maria (middle, second row) with her parents, sister Jackie, and friends in New York. Maria was always kept rather in the background in the family, like Cinderella. Her mother doted on her firstborn child, Jackie.

13

Pannain was revered and listened to by one and all. His judgments were quoted by colleagues as if they were oracles. Yet Pannain never once expressed an openly positive judgment of Callas. He was forced to admit that she was talented, but always had reservations. Even when she interpreted *Norma*, an opera in which she made her mark in history, he wrote: "It is too evident that Callas has made an unnatural adaptation to this role. Her voice is somewhat veiled and opaque, detached and formless, spoiling every outcome and creating an obstacle between her and the character...... Norma is not a role for her." He had the same negative impression in reviewing *Traviata*, the opera in which today Callas is considered an unmatchable interpreter. "She undoubtedly has an exceptional voice but should forget about *La Traviata*. Her effort in singing is unnaturally expressive, so that her voice becomes rough and sharp, cloudy, undramatic, inhuman, and unaffectionate. Violetta is a soul, not a sampler of vocal chords. She sings of her life amidst the bitterness of contrasts which consume and liberate her, and Callas does not have the temperament to make this role hers."

In the wake of Pannain, there followed other famous critics, such as Andrea Della Corte, Franco Abbiati, Alceo Toni and, especially, Beniamino Dal Fabbro, whose every word was full of poison and adversity. He judged Callas to be inadequate in all her roles. Having heard her sing *Norma*, he wrote: "Callas as a singer is too unequal in all registers, too imprecise in phrasing, too impulsive in rhythm ever to hope to be a fortunate interpreter of the tragic role of the druidess." He even denigrated her when singing Mozart. This was his comment on her performance in the *Rape of the Lock*: "Whatever was pertinent to Mozart has been entirely compromised by the forced and unpleasant, stylistically clumsy, virtuosically blurred voice of Maria Callas." He also ravaged her *Gioconda* at La Scala in December 1952: "Callas has had ample opportunity to tire herself, as well as sensitive listeners, of her prodigal 'unhedonistic emissions' (as would only be said by someone who does not understand that

methodically spoiling an entire lyrical repertoire as well as the tastes of the public." But these critics proved ineffective and left no trace behind them. The greatness of Maria obscured them all. The more time passes, the more we rediscover that her interpretative intuitions were classically linear and perfect, almost authentically genial.

The biographical story of Maria Callas is gray, if not poor and squalid. As we have said, she was born on December 4, 1923 at Flower Hospital, New York. Her Greek parents had emi-

'hedonistic emissions' refers to organs other than the throat, i.e., something unpleasant and unmannerly)." He had the same to say about Elizabeth in

grated to the United States four months earlier. Her mother, Evangelia, was twenty-four, while her father, George Kalogeropoulos, a pharmacist, was thir-

"Child prodigies never enjoy true childhood.
I can't remember a toy I cared about more than any
other—a doll or a favorite game—but only the songs I sang
and sang and sang to the point of boredom. . ."

Verdi's *Don Carlos*: "Callas is becoming something of a compulsory stage figure at La Scala, but she unfortunately never changes her costume: Her singing is the usual forced interpretation through the octaves which she poorly exploits,

ty-six. They had married in 1916 and already had two children: Giacinta, known as Jackie, born in 1917, and Vasily, born in 1920, who died a year later during the typhus epidemic.

The Kalogeropoulos's, marriage,

15

The nurses waited to find out the girl's name to write it on a bracelet so that she wouldn't be confused with the others in the nursery. But Evangelia and her husband George had never considered the possibility of having another girl and didn't have a name ready. "Call her Sofia," said Evangelia distractedly. "No, Cecilia is better," said George. The nurses wrote "Sofia Cecilia" on the bracelet. The little girl was later called Maria and, when she was baptized three years later, she was given four names: Cecilia, Sofia, Anna, Maria.

The birth of Maria Callas cannot be traced in the New York Records Office. The records of births in the first ten days of December 1923 equally do not mention a girl named Cecilia Sofia Anna Maria Kalogeropoulos, nor do the records of Flower Hospital detail her birth. It seems her parents were so disappointed that she was a girl rather than a boy that they forgot to register her birth officially.

Maria Callas herself was never sure of her exact date of birth. Dr. Leonidas Lantzounis, who saw her come into the world and was later her godfather, always maintained that she was born on December 2. Her mother always claimed that December 4 was her birth date. School records indicate December 3. Maria, when she was famous, wrote in a biographical note: "I saw the light in New York, born under the sign of Sagittarius, on the morning of December 2nd or 4th. I can't be sure about this, as for many of the circumstances of my life, since my passport declares I was born on the 2nd while my mother maintains I came into the world on the 4th. . . I prefer December 4th because, naturally, I have to believe what my mother says and also because it is the day dedicated to Saint Barbara, patron of the artillery, a proud and combative saint of whom I am very fond."

So, Maria Callas was not exactly received enthusiastically when she arrived in this world. This may seem an insignificant detail; but, in all truth, for some quirk of destiny, that rejection became the leitmotif of Callas's entire life. She always felt unwanted, both in private and professional spheres. She often succumbed to the insult and sadness of feeling like an intruder. For most of her life, she had to strive to make her way as both a woman and an artist.

"Time is a great healer," said Athenian historian Thucydides in the

which seemed authentically based on true love, was under stress right from the first year because of George's somewhat flippant behavior, a situation which aggravated familial relations when Vasily died. The decision to emigrate to America was made by both George and Evangelia in the hope that the new faraway country would help them rediscover the serenity and strength to continue living together.

Evangelia never really recovered from the death of Vasily, especially because he was a boy, a matter of enormous importance for a Greek woman of the 1920s. When she realized she was pregnant again, she immediately thought that Vasily would be reincarnated in the new life she carried in her womb. This conviction was so deeply rooted that she always spoke of the son she was going to bear, prepared clothes for a boy, and even chose a name: Vasily, of course.

When a daughter was born, she was hugely disappointed.

The doctor on duty that day when Evangelia gave birth was another Greek, a friend of the Kalogeropouloses, Dr. Leonidas Lantzounis. He presented the newborn girl to Evangelia and heard the mother's awful words of rejection: "I don't want to see her." Later, Dr. Lantzounis became a dear friend of Maria Callas, one of the few people she always cared for.

fourth century B.C. As the days went by, Evangelia resigned herself to her new daughter and the disappointment of not having another boy. Her maternal instincts came to the fore and Maria was welcomed into the family and cared for affectionately. Yet, in her heart, Evangelia was always marked by this disappointment, and Maria somehow understood that she was not wholly loved by her mother.

Maria was always left a little on the fringe of the family. She was Cinderella, the afterthought. Her mother's attention and favors always went to elder sister Jackie.

Jackie showed great musical gifts and her mother insisted that she have music lessons. Maria also studied music but always in the shadow of her sister. Whenever friends and relatives visited, it was always Jackie who was invited to

Kalogeropoulos family experienced hours and hours of indescribable anxiety. Then the doctors said that the little girl was responding well to treatment and was out of danger. She stayed in the hospital for twenty-two days, but the consequences of the accident remained with her for a considerable time.

In the same year, Maria started school. Her primary school education coincided with the Great Depression, which struck America at the end of 1929. The nation experienced an enormous crisis. George Kalogeropoulos was forced to sell his pharmacy and work as an employee. The family had to move to a cheaper apartment and later to an even poorer home.

There were financial problems at home, and it was precisely the lack of money which caused the Kalogeropouloses to argue more and more fre-

"In America, my father decided to simplify the pronunciation of our surname, Kalogeropoulos into Callas.

show off how good she was at the piano. Maria almost never had this opportunity. So, little Maria acted like a grown-up: When her sister had finished her piece and received her applause, Maria sat at the piano herself, even if not asked to do so, and played. She was fighting to survive, not to be crushed. She didn't accept the role of Cinderella. These struggles at home made her very stubborn, strong, and persevering. She suffered, but she didn't give up.

Maria was almost morbidly fond of her sister. Jackie, six years her senior, was her idol, the example to copy, the target to reach. Jackie was good, attractive, and older: everything Maria wanted to be.

In July 1929, Maria was almost killed. She was nearly six. One day, she went for a walk with her sister and parents. Jackie was walking alone, ahead of the others, in the middle of the street. Maria ran up to her with her arms open. A car appeared suddenly at high speed, hitting her and dragging her a dozen yards or so along the road.

Her father took her immediately to nearby St. Elizabeth's Hospital, where the doctors said she was seriously injured and unlikely to survive. The

quently. George wanted his wife to stop leading a lifestyle beyond their financial means. She would not accept this. They drifted further and further apart.

Maria, forced to change home and school, continually lost her friends. She had always had few friends and even these, as the family moved, became fewer. She grew more than a little ungainly in physique. Compared with children of her own age, she was tall and fat. She felt uncomfortable. The boys never stopped to chat with her. At home, she had three canaries and they became her favorite friends and secret confidants.

She sought gratification in studying and singing. She played the piano and sang popular songs. She was practically self-taught. But she showed an enormous vocation for music and had an extraordinary voice.

One day, when she was about ten years old, she was singing, accompanying herself on the pianola, "La Paloma," a popular song at the time. It was spring and the windows of the apartment were open. At one point her mother looked out into the street and realized that a small crowd had formed under their windows to listen to Maria. It was at

that moment that Evangelia realized her daughter had exceptional vocal gifts and decided that she should become a singer.

But Evangelia was in a hurry. She was ambitious and wanted her daughter to become immediately famous, so that she herself could bask in glory and, through the success of her daughter, sat-

childhood. I can't remember a toy I cared about more than any other—a doll or a favorite game—but only the songs I sang and sang and sang to the point of boredom for the school show at the end of the year. And, especially, the painful sensation of panic which seized me when, in the middle of a difficult passage, I felt as if I were going to suffo-

peak of her success. "Life is suffering and anyone who says the opposite to their children is dishonest and wicked. . . Life is a struggle without end. It is the same for everyone. Only our weapons are different and those used to our detriment. This is destiny, a mixture of personal factors and outside circumstances."

"I hated school, I hated everything and everyone. Life is suffering and anyone who says the opposite to their children is dishonest and wicked. . .Life is a struggle without end. It is the same for everyone. Only our weapons are different. . ."

isfy her own vanity. She thus took Maria to all the competitions, all the shows, all the radio programs, forcing her to sing at recitals, charity concerts, and gala evenings.

Maria made a name for herself, won prizes, competitions, and astonished everyone; but she felt she was a kind of monster, an attraction. She suffered terribly from the continual public performances. Many years later, recalling those times, she had these bitter words to say: "Child prodigies never enjoy true

cate and thought, terrorized, that no notes would emerge from my dry and arid throat. Nobody ever noticed my anxiety. . . There ought to be a law forbidding such things. Children treated in such a way become old before their time. It is unfair to deprive children of their infancy. I felt I was loved only when I sang."

Maria Callas did not have a happy childhood. She was even ill-at-ease at school. "I hated school. I hated everything and everyone," she wrote at the

Opposite page, top:

1941. Maria Callas with some Italian soldiers fighting in Greece. Singing airs from Italian operas, Maria became famous with the troops and even became engaged to a lieutenant who often went to see her with gifts of food. He helped her through the food shortages which hit Greece for the duration of the War.

Opposite page, bottom:

1942. Maria Callas (first right) with a cousin, her mother, sister Jackie, and Jackie's fianceé, on holiday in Saloniko.

Top:

1939. Maria Callas in Athens showing a fellow student of the conservatory one of the canaries she had brought with her from New York and of which she was extremely fond.

Bottom:

1944. Maria in the garden of her house. At the end of the War, she was accused of collaborating because she had given concerts for the invading soldiers and had worked for the British. She was forced to leave Greece and return to the United States.

In 1937, the marriage of Maria's parents finally disintegrated. Evangelia decided to leave New York and return to Greece with her daughters. George did not try to oppose her.

Before leaving, Maria celebrated her eighth-grade graduation. On the occasion, all the students wrote a message in a book of mementoes. Maria wrote a little verse: "Being no poet, having no fame, permit me just to sign my name."

The monthlong journey to Greece was made on the Italian ship *Saturnia*, which left New York in early February.

Life on board was happy. There were parties every evening. There was a piano and even a small orchestra. But Maria was uninterested in all this. By day, she practiced the piano and sang. Some passengers interested in music overheard her and were struck by her talent. They spoke to the captain, who asked her to sing during the religious services, but she refused. She accepted, however, an invitation to sing at a party a few days later.

She did not like drawing attention to herself. She spent most of her time with her three best friends: David, Stephanakos, and Elmina—the three canaries in a cage. They were like people for her. She especially loved David. As she admitted when older, the little bird was her best singing master. Maria spent hours on end listening and watching. She wondered how such a tiny creature could sing all those notes, with astonishing agility and spontaneity. She wanted to imitate the canary, become like him. David even sang when Maria took him in her hands. She liked to

our surname, Kalogeropoulus. I don't know whether this involved any special legal procedures. I remember that even at school I was always called Mary Callas. In Greece, on the other hand, I became Maria Kalogeropoulos again. When I arrived in Greece, I was just thirteen years old. But I looked a lot older because I was tall, strong, and rather too serious, in both looks and manner, for my age."

Maria remained in Greece from 1937 to 1945, from thirteen to twenty-

place two fingers around its neck, wanting to feel the movements of its throat and extort the canary's technical secrets. She listened and reflected. We don't know what she deduced from the solitary reflections, which even continued while she was at the conservatory in Athens. One day, when older, speaking of her singing studies in Greece, Callas said: "I learned more from David (the canary) than from all my professors at the conservatory."

"In America," she said, "my father decided to simplify the pronunciation of

one years of age. It was the golden age of her musical training, although she was not a tranquil student.

Students had to be sixteen to enter the conservatory and Maria was only thirteen. "My mother initially tried to enroll me in Athens Conservatory, the most important in all Greece," wrote Callas later. "But they laughed in her face. What could they ever do with a thirteen-year-old girl, they asked. So, pretending to be sixteen, I entered another conservatory, the National, where I began studying with a teacher

who was probably originally from Italy, Mrs. Maria Trivella."

She was a diligent student, but not entirely at ease. She rarely concerned herself with her professors or fellow students. But she was very talented. She won first prize as the best student and made her theatrical debut. "In October or November 1938, I made my stage debut," she wrote later. "For the first time, when I was not yet fifteen years old, I went on-stage in the authoritative role of prima donna. My part was Santuzza, in *Cavalleria Rusticana* and

everything went perfectly. But I was desperate because a terrible toothache caused my face to swell and become distorted. It has always been like this. At every important stage in my career, I

floors, made the beds, dusted the furniture, and prepared the meals. She didn't complain, but she was unhappy.

At that time, she also had the dis-

"At every important stage in my career, I have always and inevitably had to pay for my triumphs personally with some kind of regret or physical illness."

have always and inevitably had to pay for my triumphs personally with some kind of regret or physical illness."

She felt alone in the family. Her sister Jackie had become a beautiful young woman and was engaged to Milton Embricos, the son of a shipping magnate. Their mother Evangelia had eyes and attentions only for Jackie. Maria, even in Greece, was still Cinderella. Jackie went to parties, receptions, on walks. She was always dressed elegantly.

Evangelia stood proudly next to Jackie, diligently playing the role of a mother overseeing her young daughter and often accompanying her to parties and dinners. Maria was left at home. When she returned from the conservatory, she washed the dishes, cleaned the

pleasure of becoming visibly overweight. Many biographers have written that she was gluttonous and could not resist good food, stuffing herself with sausages, cheese, and sweets. This is entirely untrue, if not shameful defamation, since Callas, with her sensitivity,

Opposite page:

1944. Maria Callas with her mother and two friends. On the back of the photo, Evangelia wrote, in Greek (inset above): "To my golden little Maria from your mummy."

Above:

1943. Maria Callas (kneeling) during a trip to Saloniko with a group of friends. Maria studied diligently in Greece, but was not always at ease. She rarely concerned herself with her professors or fellow students.

Below:

Maria Callas (left) with her mother and sister. In the following years, once she had become a famous opera singer, Callas made bitter accusations about her mother, claiming that, while they were in Greece, she always favored her sister Jackie, then engaged to the son of a wealthy shipping magnate.

Pages 22-23:

An evocative snapshot of Maria Callas on deck.

21

HOVEN "FIDELIO"

her deep artistic feeling, her great dignity, was certainly not the kind of person to let herself go in such an uncontrolled manner. She had a noble soul and would never have devoured sausages as many writers claim. On the contrary, food did not really interest her. This is why she always protested indignantly about these legendary stories, which were even published in *Time* when she was at the peak of her fame. "At times, in the morning," she wrote, "I went out without even having a cup of tea and my mother ran after me down the stairs to give me a piece of toast to take to school. I became fat because I was treated to a diet of scrambled eggs, which

"I owe all my artistic, stage, and musical preparation and training to Elvira De Hidalgo. This wonderful woman gave me not only all her precious teaching, but also all her heart, and witnessed my entire life in Athens, both in art and in the family."

probably caused some kind of hormonal imbalance. My mother never really looked after me."

This hormonal problem was serious and had an enormous effect on Maria's life. She had a very interesting face with

deep-set, intelligent, and large eyes. But for years, especially in adolescence and as a young woman, her face was awkward and without grace. These were the years when her heart exploded with sentiment. The years of tenderness, confidences. She had no friends, no companions who gazed at her enchantedly.

She met Elvira De Hidalgo, a

famous Spanish singer then forty-seven years old, in 1938. It was a significant meeting. Contrary to what many people believe, Elvira De Hidalgo was not a singing teacher. She was only a former singer, and until she met Maria Callas had never taught her art. She had enjoyed a stunning career. In 1908, just sixteen years old, De Hidalgo made her operatic debut interpreting the part of Rosina in Rossini's *Barber of Seville* alongside the great Titta Rutto. Before she was twenty, she had audiences all over the world at her feet. She appeared onstage at the Metropolitan in New York alongside none other than Enrico Caruso. In 1916, she was chosen by Toscanini for the part of Rosina again in *Barber of Seville* at La Scala to celebrate the centennial of Rossini's opera. Between 1920 and 1930, Europe and America witnessed even more of De Hidalgo's memorable triumphs. She retired, still young, in 1930.

In 1939 she married for the second time, to a Frenchman, and was on holiday in Greece when war broke out. France had begun to engage in battle against the Germans, who had invaded Greece, and it was impossible to return home. Friends, aware of her fame and exceptional technical knowledge, invited her to teach at the Odeon Athenon Conservatory.

Elvira De Hidalgo was a very great light soprano and an exceptional singing teacher; for these reasons, she has earned a place in music history. As a singer, she entirely deserves her fame. She collected triumph after triumph in all the leading theaters, including La Scala in Milan. The same cannot really be said, however, for her performance as a teacher. She probably merely had the fortune to teach a very great pupil—

Maria Callas. In all truth, De Hidalgo may not deserve all the credit she's received. She never trained any other young singer destined for such astonishing success.

But for Callas, she was incomparably precious. She really did boast great technical gifts and experience of incalculable value. In Maria Callas she found a young woman gifted with exceptional receptive capacity and unique vocal qualities. They established a perfect understanding, and it was easy for De Hidalgo to convey everything she knew. The outcome was sensational.

"I owe all my artistic, stage, and musical preparation and training to this illustrious Spanish artist", Callas wrote. "This wonderful woman not only gave me all her precious teaching but also all her heart and witnessed my entire life in Athens, both in art and in the family".

The meeting between Maria Callas

and Elvira De Hidalgo took place in 1939, when the academic year had already begun. This demonstrates that Maria Callas was not fully at ease at the National Conservatory.

"She didn't create a good impression," De Hidalgo wrote later. "The girl was tall, fat, a little clumsy, and her face was spotted with large pimples. She was dressed simply, almost negligently. I agreed to listen to her sing. When she started, I was completely taken aback. Her voice was rough but powerful, with a very personal and extraordinary timbre."

They immediately established a friendly relationship. Elvira De Hidalgo presented the young woman to the other teachers to receive their consent for her to study at the Odeon Athenon. But they knew Maria Callas well; they knew she had studied at the other conservatory, and opposed her admission. "They told me," Elvira De Hidalgo was to say, "to forget the entire episode because the girl would only have caused trouble for me. She is 'aloof,' they said, disparagingly."

Who knows what Maria had done to earn such a reputation. She was in a delicate position. It would have become impossible for her to study. And this was when Elvira De Hidalgo intervened, almost miraculously. The great singer intuitively realized that Maria Callas was singularly gifted. Against everyone else's opinion, and at the risk of arousing dangerous enmities, she opened her arms to her. She said to her teaching colleagues: "Let's not speak of this any more. I'll take on this pupil at my own expense, you will not have to worry about paying me for the lessons I shall give her."

Maria thus did not attend the new conservatory as a regular student, but on a private basis as the personal student of Elvira De Hidalgo, who gave her lessons free of charge.

Elvira De Hidalgo was a true mother figure for Maria Callas, the kind of caring and affectionate mother the girl had never known. She conveyed to Maria all of her technical and artistic knowledge, as well as wisdom and advice about how to overcome life's many difficulties.

Maria was extremely fond of De Hidalgo. She was always with her teacher. "She wasn't like my other pupils, who came when it was their turn for lessons and went immediately afterwards," De Hidalgo told. "Maria, always in silence, almost sulkily, arrived at ten in the morning, when I began my lessons, sat in a corner, and stayed there until I had finished, towards the evening. She followed the lessons of all the pupils and learned everything. She had an incredible memory and frightening determination. When her turn came, she studied with me. For the rest of the day, she didn't say one word to me. After a few weeks, she asked if she could accompany me home in the evening. And we came to stay even more together. As we walked, she continually asked for advice and explanations. At the beginning, I thought it was merely a passing enthusiasm. But she always maintained the same, almost desperate dedication."

At the end of 1940, the War engulfed Greece. German and Italian troops occupied Athens, and its inhabitants suffered from the accompanying restrictions. A curfew was imposed; cinemas, theaters, concert halls were closed. Basic necessities were almost impossible to find. The people went hungry and the black market appeared. The people of Athens were forced to make long and dangerous nighttime excursions into the country to find food. Maria herself experienced these sacrifices.

"I remember the winter of 1941," she wrote. "Greece was invaded by the Germans and the people had already been starving for many months. It had never been so cold in Athens. For the first time in twenty years, the Athenians

have meant the firing squad, since the Germans were inexorable. Yet I never returned empty-handed. But in the winter of 1941, a friend of the family, at that time engaged to my sister, came to us with a little barrel of olive oil, maize flour and potatoes. I shall never forget the incredulous astonishment with which I, my mother, and Jackie gazed at these precious items, as if frightened

that some magic spell could have whisked them away at any moment."

The soldiers were always looking for young girls. Those who were kind

It is impossible to be sure, but there is evidence to suggest that she may well have been involved. Leading film director Franco Zeffirelli, who was Maria's very close friend, made some confidential remarks to us, revealing episodes which nobody knows about, but which Callas herself confirmed. "During the War, Callas was seventeen," remarked Zeffirelli. "She was good-looking,

"I remember the winter of 1941. . . Greece was invaded by the Germans and the people had already been starving for many months. We were rehearsing Tiefland and had to perform in the semi-darkness, barely lit by acetylene lamps for fear of the bombings."

saw snow. We were rehearsing *Tiefland* and had to perform in the semi-darkness, barely lit by acetylene lamps for fear of the bombings. For the entire summer, I had only eaten tomatoes and boiled cabbage, which I was able to find only by walking for miles and miles into the country to persuade the people there to give me something to eat. For them, a basket of tomatoes and cabbage could

received pasta, rice, bread, chocolate, and coffee in exchange. Temptation and necessity were great. In appearance, everything was played as a game, an idyllic and innocent friendliness. But the truth was much closer to prostitution. The girls, essentially, gave themselves to the soldiers in exchange for food.

Did Maria Callas succumb to this?

although a little plump. There was nothing to eat, and the people went hungry. To survive, you either bought food on the black market or did the best you could. Evangelia had two daughters and did the best she could to get by. Maria sang, and her mother expected that she went out every evening to entertain the soldiers and earn food in return. But Maria immediately realized that the solidiers were not at all interested in music but wanted something else from her. She tried to explain it all to her mother, who refused to be reasonable. Every afternoon, the two women had furious rows. "No, I'm not going," said Maria, crying. But Evangelia threw her out of the house telling her not even to attempt to come back without something to eat.

All these things were told to me by an eyewitness, Greek painter Jan Tsaroukis, who lived in Athens in the apartment next-door to the Callas family. He heard their arguments, heard Maria leave slamming the door, looked out of the window, and saw that she was not going off to the soldiers. She waited in a little square nearby for a young Italian soldier to arrive, with whom she was secretly engaged. They stayed together and chatted. Every now and then, Maria would sing for him. 'They were very touching and tender scenes,' Tsaroukis told me.

"When I became friends with Maria, I spoke of this to her. She looked at me indignantly. 'How did you find out about this?' she asked me. 'Who told you? Did you know that soldier?' 'No, it was one of your neighbors who saw you from the window,' I answered. Maria was thoughtful for a moment and then said: 'You wicked man, you were spying on me before we even met!' She paused and then added: 'You now know a secret in my life that no one else has ever heard about.'"

Elvira De Hidalgo was also a witness to these brutal times and realized the dangers into which Maria might have fallen. She did what she could to avoid them. She used all her influence and important connections to obtain for her pupil a permanent place in the State Opera chorus. This meant Maria had a salary, and therefore was not forced to make ends meet, to seek the help of soliders with other desires.

Elvira De Hidalgo also wanted Maria to gain stage experience. At the end of her first year of training, in 1940, De Hidalgo assigned Callas the role of Suor Angelica in Puccini's opera for the school's end-of-year exhibition. In 1941, she performed in Suppé's operetta *Boccaccio*. In 1942, she prepared Maria for an important debut: a prestigious opera, *Tosca*, set up by professionals.

Accounts of this debut vary. It has been written that the leading lady in the opera was supposed to be a well-known singer in Athens who was not exactly young anymore. This singer was taken ill, and Maria Callas was called to take her place. The famous singer hated the young Callas, precisely because she was talented and thus capable of definitively overshadowing her own reputation. The older singer simply could not let this happen and even sent her husband to prevent the debut. There followed a violent argument. Maria defended herself with her fingernails and ruined the poor man's face. But she received several violent punches and, consequently, appeared onstage with a black eye.

It was a spicy little episode indeed, and one often published in the press, including *Time* magazine, when Maria was the reigning queen of international opera; it has also been repeated many times in biographies. Callas attempted more than once, unsuccessfully, to deny the whole fracas. When *Time* republished the story in 1956, she wrote in protest to the editor: "It's not true that I was called upon at the last moment to sing Tosca in place of a colleague. The opera was staged for me and we rehearsed for three months. Dino Janopoulos can prove this because he was the director. The story of the torn shirt, the black eye and the husband's bloody nose is a complete invention. All lies. It is not even true that the critics were enthusiastic about my performance. They have never spoken well of me." It is true that certain critics were reserved in their praise. Sofia Spanudi,

the music critic of *Athinaikà Néa*, wrote: "Miss Maria Kalogeropoulos, pupil of the famous artist De Hidalgo, was given the demanding role of Tosca. 'Was given' in this context is a clarification: She is a young and still inexperienced artist, and if her musical creation did not fall to pieces in the course of interpreting this exacting role, then this is great praise for her. She 'was not' Tosca as such, but even now we can be sure she will be one day. She has stage craft and presence, and a rich voice, which has not yet crystallized into the scope of the dramatic soprano."

However, other critics did write favorable reviews, such as Dr. Coulmas: "Maria Kalogeropoulos gave Tosca a fine and convincing stage presence, at the same time as making the desired woman

and the famous woman credible. Her voice and its easy modulations were equally excellent."

Alexandra Lalauni: "We should speak with the highest praise of the very young singer, Maria Kalogeropoulos, who interpreted Tosca in such a surprising way. We should simply bear in mind that this young singer is only eighteen, taking the stage for the first time in such a difficult role, turning Puccini's tragic heroine into flesh and blood with so much passion and so much truth to the point of believing she created a real, living human being."

As we can see, only Spanudi expressed certain reservations. The other critics praised Maria, yet she was profoundly struck by the negative

reviews and remembered only these.

Stage training under the guidance of Elvira De Hidalgo continued. In 1943, Maria Callas resumed the recitals of *Tosca* and sang in a number of concerts. In 1944 she sang in *Tiefland* by Eugen d'Albert, in *Cavalleria Rusticana* by Pietro Mascagni and *Fidelius* by Beethoven.

"In the summer of 1944, I had my first clashes with colleagues," wrote Maria. "We were staging *Fidelius*. Another prima donna had made strenuous efforts to win the part and finally received it. But she had made no effort to learn it. Since rehearsals had to start straightaway, I was asked if I could step in and, naturally, I accepted because I knew the part perfectly. I say all this to demonstrate that my only weapon, a

very powerful and honest weapon, is always to be well-prepared, since no amount of favoritism can stand up to skill. Before the curtain goes up, everything can be done to support an artist. But when the curtain goes up, only ability speaks. They say that I always win. These are my methods: hard work and preparation."

Maria's success in this opera was beyond comparison. The opera was staged on August 14 in the Herodus Atticus Amphitheater. The War was drawing to an end. The Germans retreated from Athens two months later. On that evening under the stars, music brought together the invaders and the

from the strain of those times, which have left me the melancholy heritage of liver problems and blood pressure of about 90 when I'm well. . .

"The Civil War broke out in Athens on December 4, 1944. The British advised me not to leave the headquarters; had my delicate task of sorting secret messages for them been discovered, I would have inevitably suffered at the hands of the Communists. But my home was located in an area controlled by the Reds and I didn't want to leave my mother on her own. I asked to be accompanied home and was taken in a jeep to Patassion Street, where I stayed in my room for a few days. I was

Opposite page, top:

A general view of the Herodus Atticus Amphitheater where, in 1944, Callas interpreted Beethoven's Fidelius. Maria achieved enormous success in this opera. It was staged on August 14 in the Herodus Atticus Amphitheater. The War was drawing to an end: The Germans retreated from Athens two months later. On that evening under the stars, music brought together the invaders and the invaded, sitting side-by-side.

Opposite page, bottom:

1941. Maria Callas in a stage photo of Suppé's opera, Boccaccio, at the Pallàs Cinema in Athens.

Side:

1944. Maria Callas in a scene from Fidelius. This opera brought her great popularity in Greece. The critics were unreservedly favorable. "Miss Kalogeropoulos dominated the awesome role in the best possible manner," wrote critic Hamudopulos.

"My only weapon, a very powerful and honest weapon, is always to be well-prepared, since no amount of favoritism can stand up to skill. Before the curtain goes up, everything can be done to support an artist. But when the curtain goes up, only ability speaks."

invaded, sitting side-by-side. The critics on this occasion were unanimous in praising the main character. Even Sofia Spanudi, who had expressed certain reservations over *Tosca*, was highly complimentary.

She wrote: "Maria Kalogeropoulos, in the immense role of Leonora, revealed a disciplined voice in the most severe Beethovian style, as well as excellent musicality and the intensity of a great artist. She was truly, on a musical level and in terms of overall performance, a worthy interpreter of this heroine's style."

She rested for some time after *Fidelius*. The Royal Opera Theater was closed. Evangelia sought and found for her daughter a job as a clerk in the British headquarters.

"I was assigned to sorting the secret messages," she wrote. "I began work at 8:00 a.m. but I had to get up at 6:30 because I walked all the way to work to save the tram fare. My house, at 61 Patission Street, was a long way from the office. At midday the British provided a good meal for us and I put it in a pot to take home to share with my mother. I had no more than an hour-and-a-half break, and could stay at home for no more than fifteen minutes. I carried on like that until winter, but I still suffer

gripped with fear. In such conditions, I couldn't think of finding something to eat for me and my mother, and I may even have starved to death (many people did in those times) if friends had not helped. Later, I had to return to the British headquarters because the Reds were looking for me and I might have been killed."

"I am a creature of de[stiny] wanted me this way. I [would] watch my life fr[om ...]

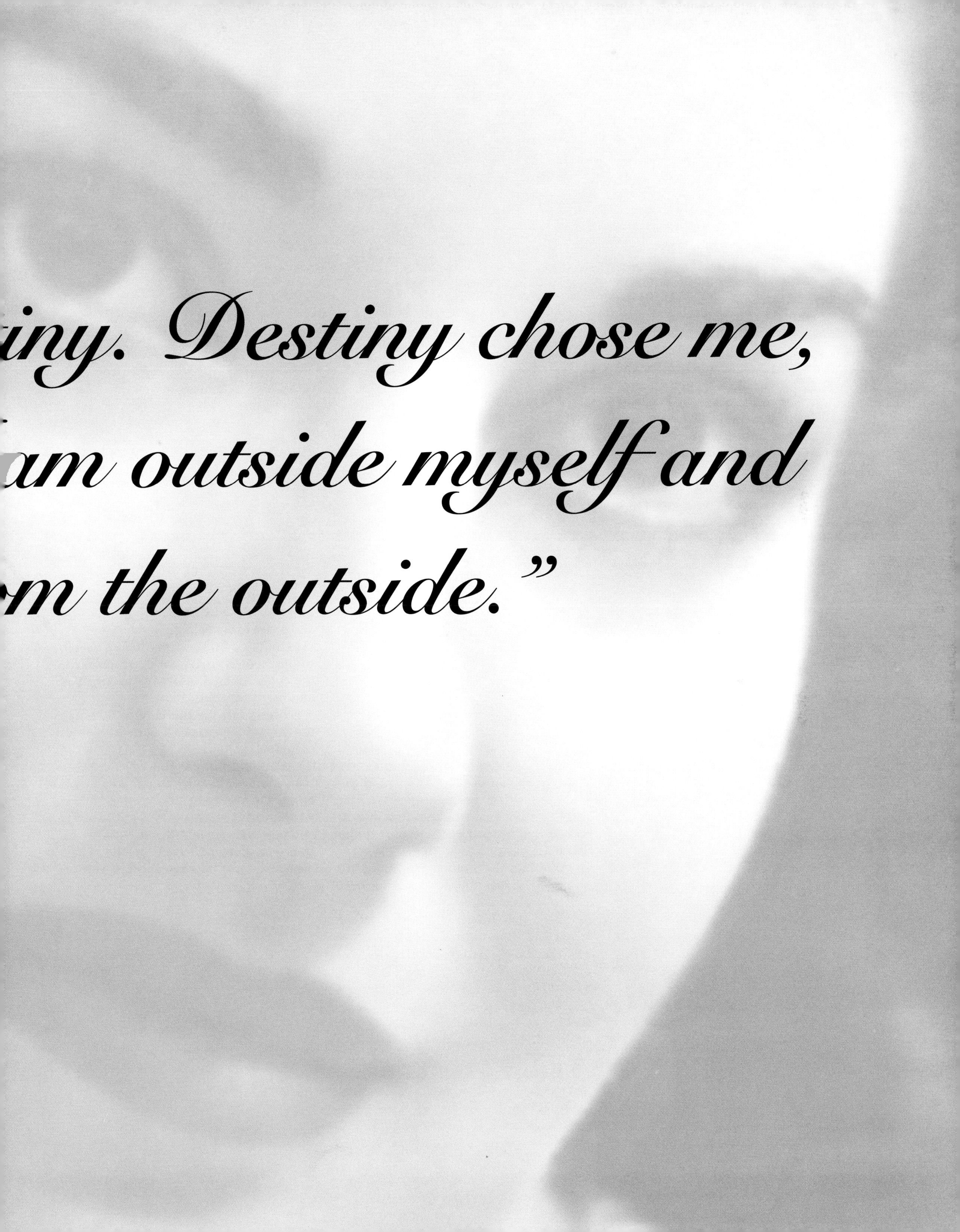

tiny. Destiny chose me,

am outside myself and

om the outside."

A new epoch began for Greece when the War ended in 1945. There was great ferment and excitement in the air, not least in the world of music.

Maria had completed her studies and had shown great skill. She had a contract with the Royal Opera Theater in Athens and could now begin her career. But the new political situation brought with it drastic changes in the management of the theater. The new managers were men of the Resistance; their first act was a great purge. All the artists untuned to the new politics were dismissed. Maria, perhaps because she had sung for the occupying troops and also because she had worked for the British, was accused of being a collaborator, and her contract was broken. She protested, but her career in Greece was over before it could even start. She would never have the chance to go onstage.

She was furious. Just as the dream of her life was about to come true, everything fell to pieces. It was a disaster. But, used to trials and tribulations,

Callas did not lose heart. "I'm going," she said to her teacher. "I shall return to the States and seek my fortune there."

Elvira De Hidalgo did not agree with this decision. She had repeated to her pupil for some time that her future could only start in Italy, the home of *bel canto*, fine singing. She had even taught her a little Italian with this in mind. In the evening, as they returned home from the conservatory, De Hidalgo talked to Maria in Italian and Callas learned the language with surprising ease. De Hidalgo tried again to convince her to leave for Italy. But Maria realized she was in no position to do so.

She had no money. She knew no one in Italy. She couldn't take the risk. The only place where she could look for help was the United States. Her father still lived there, but she didn't know exactly where. George had cut off all relations with the family in 1937, but Maria knew that he was very fond of her. The two of them had always understood each other perfectly, and she was sure that she would find him, and that he would help her.

She told her family that she was leaving for New York but gave no other explanations. The mayor of Pireus wanted to give her a farewell dinner. Maria accepted willingly but did not want either her mother or sister at her side. Equally, she did not want her mother and sister to accompany her to the quayside on the evening of her final goodbye to her homeland. These episodes make the relationships between the soprano and her family quite clear.

Maria left for the United States at the end of September on the passenger ship *Stockholm*.

She had bought the ticket with a loan made to her by the U.S. government. On the quayside of the port of Athens that evening, only Elvira De Hidalgo was present for the last goodbyes—the talented teacher who had also been an affectionate mother-figure.

Opposite page, bottom:

1944. A portrait photo of Jackie Callas, Maria's elder sister. While Maria made her name as a singer in Athens, Jackie began a career as a concert pianist.

Opposite, top:

1944. Maria, standing center, with the chorus of Fidelius.

Side:

1944. Maria Callas in the role of Leonora, the main character in Fidelius, disguised as a soldier trying to find her husband.

Top:

1944. Another snapshot of Jackie Callas, Maria's sister.

Debut in Ver

Maria Callas made her debut on August 2, 1947 in the Arena at Verona. It was the first time Callas sang in a theater outside Greece. Thus, it was her official debut in the world of opera.

La Gioconda, the masterpiece by Amilcare Ponchielli, was chosen that year to inaugurate the first true opera festival season in Verona after the War. The other two operas in the program were Gounod's *Faust* and *Un Ballo in Maschera* by Verdi.

La Gioconda was directed by Tullio Serafin, one of the great conductors and by no means a lesser figure than Toscanini, especially in the field of opera. The male protagonist was Richard Tucker, who was to become one of the great tenors of the century; he was also making his debut at the Arena.

Maria Callas was not quite twenty-four years old. This debut meant everything to her—all her dreams and life itself. If the debut flopped, she would have been forced to abandon her stage

career and made to return to America to find a job. After having left Greece in 1945 in search of fame and fortune, she had not enjoyed much success. She looked for parts in the United States, trying out her voice and auditioning, but everything went wrong. She didn't sing in a single concert in two years.

She had been chosen for a part in *Turandot*, being staged in Chicago, and even went through all the rehearsals. She was hoping to be successful since the cast included many well-known artists, such as Mafalda Favero, Galliano Masini, and Luigi Infantino. But just one week before the curtain was to go up, the organizer fled without paying anyone. To pay for the return flight to New York, Maria had to ask friends for a loan.

Yet the part at the Arena in Verona emerged precisely from this mishap. With her in the cheated cast was Nicola Rossi Lemeni, a young Veronese opera singer with an extraordinary bass voice

ona

who was destined for a great career. He immediately recognized the quality of Callas's voice and promised to help her.

Before leaving New York, Rossi Lemeni paid a visit to a well-known tenor, Giovanni Zenatello, also from Verona, who lived in the city. He was the originator of the Arena Opera Season. It was thanks to his intuition in 1913 that the magnificent Roman amphitheater became such an astonishing setting for lyric opera. He verified the excellent acoustics and organized with friends the first legendary events which continued until 1939, when the outbreak of war brought the seasons to an end.

But, now, the War was over and the Arena resumed its programs. The Veronese organizers turned to Zenatello to ask for his help in finding good singers on a low budget, since funds were very limited. They were especially looking for a soprano able to tackle the difficult role of Gioconda in Ponchielli's opera. Zenatello contacted Arturo Toscanini, who recommended one of his favorites, the soprano Herva Nelly. But Nelly, sure of the support of her famous mentor, asked for far more money than the Arena would spend. Zenatello found himself in a quandary. "I know the ideal soprano for Gioconda," Rossi Lemeni told him, mentioning the name of Maria Callas. "Never heard of her," Zenatello replied, but still decided to give her an audition. And Callas convinced him.

Zenatello made her sign a Spartan contract. Callas had an impressive voice, but she was unknown. He offered her forty thousand lire for each recital. This was especially modest, since only four nights were scheduled. Generally, travel and accommodation are paid for by the organizers, but Zenatello even excluded these expenses from the contract with Callas. For a fee of just 160,000 lire, Maria had to pay for her transatlantic crossing and about two months' hotel accommodation in Italy.

There would be nothing left. It was the breadline. But it was providential for Callas and she agreed enthusiastically.

Maria travelled to Italy on a Swedish cargo ship. She was accompanied by a friend, Louise, the wife of a lawyer, Eddie Bagarozy, who acted as an agent for opera singers. In all truth, he was not exactly a great manager because in two years of residence in the United States he hadn't found a single role for Maria Callas.

However, he had a soft spot for Maria. There had been some tenderness between them. Although details are unknown, they certainly had some kind of relationship.

We shall see later how this episode

became extremely important when Callas was at the peak of her fame, to the extent of becoming an international scandal. To keep everything quiet, Callas was obliged to fork out huge sums of money.

It was an adventure that throws light on an unknown and curious side of the singer. In the two years in America when she simply could not find any roles, Maria, as we shall see in some of her letters, did not let herself become sad or desperate but rather enjoyed herself and had a number of flirtations. She had a group of friends who might be considered rebels against convention, free of preconceptions, idlers, ironic, and with few scruples. She had ended up, in a certain sense, among singers on the fringes of society—a group plagued

by failures and disappointments. She had even been betrayed and ignored by these friends, but this didn't cause her too much heartache.

When Zenatello offered her a contract, she was especially happy because the contract itself was a kind of revenge for her. Lawyer Bagarozy immediately contacted her. Until that time, he had absolutely no contract with Callas. Their

agreements were only verbal. But now, scenting money, the lawyer dashed to get her signature on a contract. Maria could have refused, pointing out that he had not attained this contract for her. But, on the contrary, she was happy because this engagement gave new life to their relationship after a period of

having drifted apart. Young Callas was thinking of her life rather than money or her career.

The contract with Bagarozy read:

"Contract stipulated on this day June 13,1947 between Mr. E. Richard Bagarozy, hereafter "the personal representative," and Miss Maria Callas, hereafter "the artist." Whereas the personal representative has obtained a contract

signed by the artist to appear as leading singer in the 1947 Summer Festival to be held in Verona, Italy, and moreover, at his own expense, has ensured that the artist has received necessary promotion and the contacts appropriate to the career she has chosen and in that the artist has agreed to appoint said personal representative as her sole and exclusive agent for a period of ten years from the date indicated above. Inasmuch, with reference to the foregoing and the reciprocal agreements contained in this contract, the parties stipulate the following:

1 - The artist hereby appoints the personal representative as sole and exclusive personal agent for a period of 10 (ten) years from the date indicated above, and agrees not to accept other engagements without the prior approval of the agent and, moreover, in accordance with this contract, confers to the agent all powers to act in her name, sign those contracts on her behalf which in the opinion of the personal representative are of particular interest to the artist.

the interest of the artist herself, the personal representative undertakes to apply his best discernment in accepting or refusing such offers.

4 - The personal representative agrees to provide the artist with legal services and advice in order to ensure that the interests of the artist are legally and technically safeguarded.

5 - In witness of the foregoing, the parties have applied their signatures and stamps on the day and year aforementioned."

Lawyer Bagarozy was nothing if not concrete. For fear of losing his interests, he sent his wife Louise to Italy with the official purpose of accompanying their friend but, in truth, to keep an eye on her income.

2 - The artist also agrees to present to the personal agent any offers made to her in the field of theatrical undertakings or the production of recordings, radio and television shows, cinema, etc., and not to accept any undertakings unless approved in advance by the per-

The two women were accompanied onboard by Nicola Rossi Lemeni and other people. These included a young Swiss man with whom Maria made friends. It was an uncomfortable crossing. "We three women had to share one cabin," Maria wrote later. "I more or less

"I kept to a strict diet in America and my weight fell

from 218 to 170 pounds."

sonal representative.

3 - The personal representative undertakes to perform his tasks assiduously and at any time in order to promote and launch the career of the artist. Moreover, the personal representative agrees to analyze and examine with due diligence all offers requesting the performance of the artist; and, moreover, in

starved. We only ate potatoes and butter and a few other awful things."

Some of the photos from this trip in Maria's private album are reproduced here.

The ship disembarked in Naples. Callas had to travel to Verona by train. In third class—the class for poor people, because she could not afford anything

"We three women had to share one cabin. I more or less starved. We only ate potatoes and butter and a few other awful things."

more comfortable. She had a shabby cardboard suitcase with all her clothes and in the confusion at the port of Naples, it was stolen. She was left with nothing. She took the train, travelling for a day and a night, with sadness in her heart. She reached Verona on the evening of June 29. She was booked at the Hotel Accademia. Since all her clothes had been stolen, she went straight to her room, where she washed her blouse and underwear, hanging them up to dry in the bathroom so that she could wear them the following day.

She was invited to dinner on June 30 with all the other singers involved in the coming opera festival. The dinner was already served when a Veronese industrialist also arrived, Giovan Battista Meneghini, an opera-lover and friend of the organizers of the Arena season. He was presented to the artists, but his gaze remained fixed on Maria Callas. The rather plump girl with deep, sad eyes, struck his heart. As he confessed later, it was love at first sight.

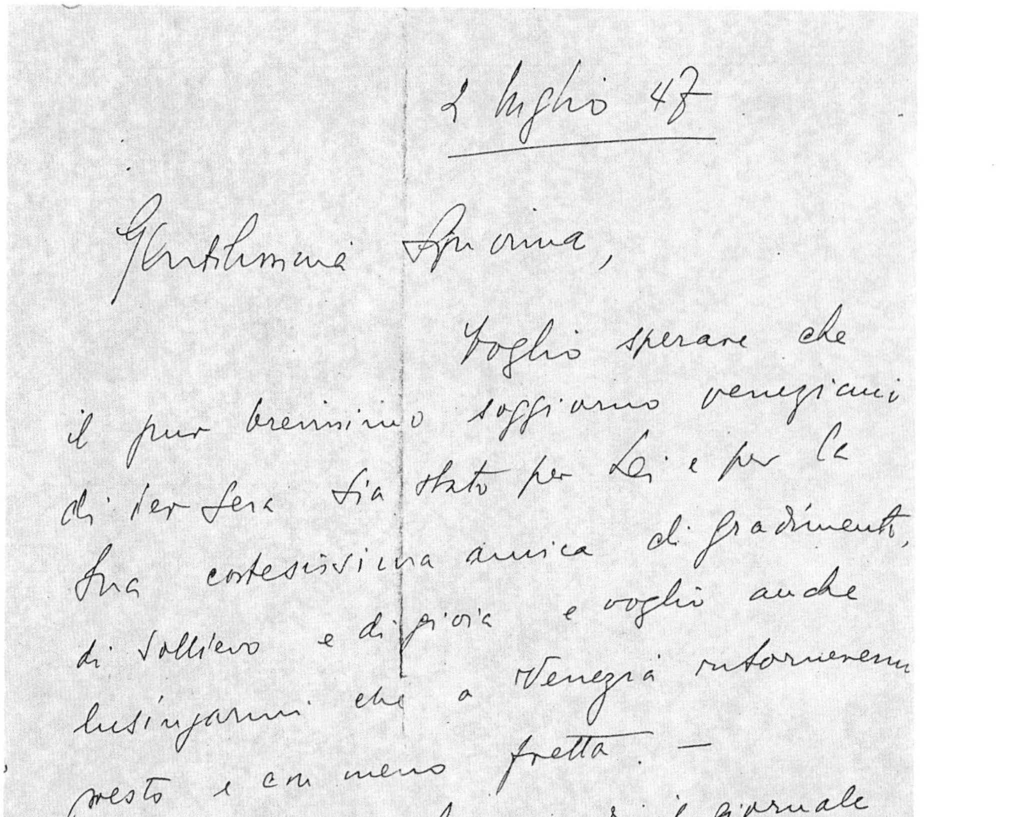

2 luglio 47

Gentilissima Signorina,

Voglio sperare che il pur brevissimo soggiorno veneziano di ier sera sia stato per Lei e per la sua cortesissima amica di gradimento, di sollievo e di gioia e voglio anche lusingarmi che a Venezia ritorneremo presto e con meno fretta. —

Le mando il giornale locale di [...]

Meneghini was fifty-two years old, twenty-nine more than Maria Callas. He was not a physically striking person: medium height, somewhat stout himself; but, he was a very capable businessman. In 1920, he inherited a brick factory from his father which, under his guidance, developed into a huge company and one of the most important in the field in Italy. In 1947, Meneghini owned twelve factories employing dozens and dozens of people.

Maria Callas was by no means beautiful and was certainly overweight. Many remarks have been made about her weight and many inaccurate things have been written. She herself wrote: "I kept to a strict diet in America and my weight fell from 218 to 170 lbs." So, she weighed 170 lbs. She was about 5' 8" tall; according to health and fitness tables, she should have weighed around 145 lbs. She was therefore still around

ed to accompany her back to the hotel. To be near her, he organized a trip to Venice the following day for all the singers. He made an appointment for 5:00 P.M. outside the Hotel Accademia. Everyone turned up punctually, except for Callas. Maria had nothing to wear and was ashamed at the idea of presenting herself in the same clothes as the evening before. Meneghini begged the director of the Arena to go and convince her and then insisted that she should travel in his car.

He courted her during the trip. Maria stayed silent but later began to confide her worries. On the way back, Meneghini stopped the car in a little square near Vicenza and kissed Callas. A love story was born.

The day after, he sent the young singer a letter.

"My dear young lady, I hope that the unfortunately short visit to Venice was, for both you and your kind friend, enjoyable, pleasurable and joyful, and I sincerely hope that we will be able to

Opposite page:

1947. Maria Callas (third from the left) with some colleagues during the opera season at the Verona Arena. Callas made her debut in Gioconda *on August 2, under conductor Tullio Serafin. Other singers were Carlo Tagliabue, Elena Nicolai, Anna Maria Canali, Richard Tucker, and Nicola Rossi Lemeni.*

Background to the photo: the first letter Giovan Battista Meneghini, the future husband of the singer, wrote to Maria Callas. It is dated July 2, three days after her arrival in Verona.

Side, left:

1947. a close-up of Maria Callas.

Side, right:

The letter which Tullio Serafin wrote at the end of the Arena season recommending Callas to Emma Moglioli, a singing teacher he trusted. The famous conductor states, among other things, that "Miss Kallas has a truly exceptional voice, which has all the scope to tackle even the most difficult roles. Strong, powerful notes and sweet and easy slow tones, a natural agility. . ."

"You are able to make me so happy with just one word or equally unhappy with just another one. You are intelligent and refined, you understand me."

twenty-five lbs. overweight, but certainly slimmer than when she was in the United States and certainly not as awkward in appearance.

During the evening, Meneghini realized that the other diners were making great fun of the Greek singer precisely because of her stature. His admiration and affection grew enormously. He want-

return to Venice soon and in less haste... "I remain your obedient servant. Please give my best regards to Louise. Sincerely, G. B. Meneghini."

It was the first of many. These letters are exceptional documents, the only true and fair testimony of what was happening around Callas and in her private life at that time.

Books usually claim that Meneghini fell in love with Callas when he heard her sing. This is quite untrue, as these letters clearly prove. When Meneghini began to write to Callas and court her, Maria had not even taken part in one rehearsal in the Arena and it was therefore impossible that Meneghini could have heard her sing. He had fallen in love with her, completely. He didn't care in the least about her voice. None of the many letters written in July and August, during the rehearsals of *Gioconda* and during the four recitals envisaged in the contract, make any mention of her voice or her singing style. It may even be that Meneghini, taken up with his own business affairs, never actually went to hear Callas sing during the rehearsals of *Gioconda*.

The legend that Meneghini became interested in Callas after hearing her sing, and that he was thus first impressed by her voice and only later by her, is probably based on a specific episode. To justify his interest in her and be close to her, Meneghini took advantage of the fact that she was in

ers I shall personally choose for you. At the end of the year, we shall assess the outcome. If we are both satisfied, we shall sign another contract to govern our future business relationships."

As we can see, the agreements were very precise and extremely advantageous for Callas. She understood this immediately and agreed willingly. She realized that, in exchange, she would have to accept the courtship of the industrialist, but Meneghini was capable, kind, and certainly knew how to make himself well-liked. That dinner at Lake Garda gave the final touch to their friendship. The day after, they were already on first name terms, as Meneghini's letters of the time clearly demonstrate.

July 6, 1947:
"My dear Maria, here is the first mail to reach you. It is not from America, but from Italy, from Verona, where you have come to bring the smile of your youth and the promise of enjoyment and joy in your art. Accept this welcome and may your smile be one of happiness and your art a source of goodness. . ."

dream. You inspire goodness in me and I make a gift of my soul to you. I embrace you with all my heart."

July 18:
"My dearest, I did not wish to leave you last night and I came back after I said goodbye but you had already gone to your room. I don't know, but my soul did not support the idea of separation, however brief, which comes to me ever more unbearably."

July 23:
"My Maria, please accept these flowers which I hope tell you of the affectionate intensity of my thoughts, thoughts always devoted to you. Last night I felt for you in such a sweet, almost inexpressible way: sweeter, dearer, more returned, more ours than ever before."

July 30:
"My Maria, a greeting and a thought to start your day. And a hope: a hope for eternal happiness, goodness, and joy. And, more, a caress, on your open brow and your hair that I like so much and makes me shiver with sweetness. It is the same caressing hand as in Venice, on the unforgettable night of the Savior. Today's newspaper speaks at length about you, in the most complimentary and kind way. It makes me happy. You deserve it all."

"For the first time, I have met my kind of man. Should I perhaps leave him and be unhappy for the rest of my life? He has everything I could ever want and adores me. It is not love, it is something more."

42

Verona for the opera season, offering to help her in her career. He told her he had contacts, possibilities, important friends in the world of opera. Since he was a shrewd businessman, he probably thought that one day the young singer would have found fame and fortune and this could have turned to his own advantage. All this, however, emerged without his really being aware of her voice and singing gifts. The "contract" binding her to him was like a blank check. And he wrote it immediately. He told Maria he had to talk to her about very important things and invited her to dinner on July 4. They went to a restaurant on Lake Garda and during the meal he illustrated his project, which he had even had typed as if dealing with a proper business arrangement.

"Until the end of the year, i.e., for the next six months, I will cover all your expenses: hotels, restaurants, clothes, everything. You shall only concern yourself with singing and studying with teach-

July 8, 1947:
"My dear Maria, it is always with great friendship and much, much tenderness that I return to you, thinking of your exquisite sensitivity and your innate, sweet kindness. In the few moments that we have been together, I would have liked to say much more to you. Not give to you, because my spirit offers you every sweetest understanding. Think of me as I think of you, with affectionate assiduousness and remember what I said to you last night: 'You live in me full of goodness and grace and I follow you with the expression of my devoted and dear soul.' Live as I ardently wish you always to live: always happy."

July 9, 1947:
"San Vigilio, Lake Garda. An enchanting evening, dreamlike and oblivious in loving peace and spiritual contact with the elect soul of a sweet young creature. Maria! Your name, your face, your eyes thrill and enchant me like a sweet

August 1:
"My dearest Maria, I send you the small Madonna I promised to you at the onset of our wonderful relationship and although I realize it is perhaps worthless in comparison with what I would like to give you, it nevertheless belongs to you and marks an unforgettable date. This is why you should accept it and keep it safe even if it is not worth so very much. Its spiritual value, on the contrary, is

moment of your art. I embrace you as you know how."

Maria made her debut in the Arena on August 2. An extremely important date, but one which is not reflected in any of Meneghini's letters. During the dress rehearsal, Maria again risked her life. As she went out onstage, she did not notice one of the small tunnels leading to the underground basements of the amphitheater and fell down inside. She sprained her ankle, which caused her great pain. She performed Gioconda

enormous, greater than any other gift I could make to you. It will bless and protect you forever, forever and forever."

August 5, three days after the opening night of *Gioconda*:
"Dearest, more flowers, the few I was able to find, to express the tenderness you inspire in me and which I always give to you, always with unchanged and immutable love. Be calm, trusting, and serene. I will accompany you in every

almost immobile onstage because she could hardly walk. Yet Meneghini was not in the audience in the Arena that evening and made no mention of the episode in his letters.

August 8:
"I will meet you at 8:30 P.M. to go to the Arena. We can have dinner after the opera, since it will hopefully be short. I should tell you that 'the skies will clear.' It's a good omen for a happy evening. I

embrace you, take you in my arms. . ."

August 14:
"My dearest, I left you awhile ago wrapped in my tenderness, which shall always be yours in ecstatic abundance. Mine more than ever, I wanted to go away, leaving you in the tremors of a divine and solemn moment all my soul. I am still near you in the tormented yearning of our passion."

Maria was distracted by this passionate and insistent courtship. She accepted it. She had immediately become Meneghini's beloved. But she didn't answer her suitor's letters. Her Italian wasn't good enough and she did not dare to try and write it. Meneghini, in any case, didn't speak a word of English.

However, we do know about her reactions and feelings from the other letters she wrote to America at the time. Letters she wrote in secret that Meneghini and her friend Louise didn't know about, to Bagarozy, her lawyer, the husband of Louise, with whom she was in also love. At that time, Callas was somewhat flippant. Her ideas and sentiments were unclear. She did her best, accepting attentions from wherever they came.

From the letters sent to Bagarozy, it appears that her feelings about Meneghini fluctuated. She moved from being in love to the point of anticipating marriage (not the least to settle her economic situation), to simply main-

ished her performances in the Arena three days beforehand. She was relaxed, probably well statisfied with her success and the attentions of Meneghini, who was still caring and ever-present.

"Dear Eddie, this morning, after two months, we finally received your letter. Naturally, I say 'we' because Louise and I have by now become a single person. I am really happy to hear that you are pulling yourself out of the trouble you were in, Eddie, and I wish the best for you with all my heart as I have always

"Thanks to God, who has given me this angelic person. . .

for the first time in my life I have no need of anyone else.

I shall think deeply about the possibility of marrying him,

I promise. But the truth is that it is so rare

to find a kindred spirit."

taining the relationship, while excluding any thought at all of marriage, since she did not feel it was true love.

The letters are amusing and lively, and clearly show that she was infatuated with both Bagarozy and Meneghini without being deeply in love with either of them.

There are three of these letters. The first is dated August 20. Maria had fin-

done and will always do, despite the fact that you have never understood me.

"Dear, I know that you complain because I do not write to you and I understand that. But you do not understand that there must have been some reason for this. In fact, I began to write you a very long letter but for certain reasons, which I will explain to you later, I decided in the end not to write to you.

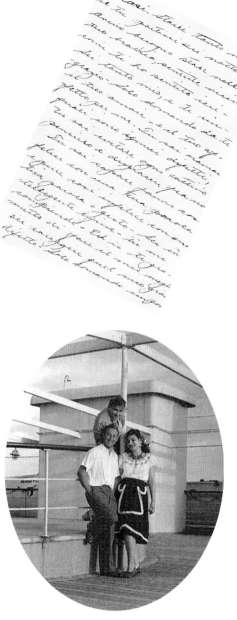

Opposite page:

1943. A full-figure portrait of Maria Callas.

Center:

1947. Maria Callas on the Rossija *cargo ship during the voyage to Italy, accompanied by lawyer Eddie Bagarozy's wife, Louise. (At the time, Callas was in love with Bagarozy.) Immediately upon arrival in Naples, where she had to take a train for Verona, Callas was robbed of all her baggage.*

Side, top:

The first letter Maria wrote to Meneghini. It is dated September 22, 1947 and was sent after a crisis that caused Callas a great deal of anxiety and tension.

Side, bottom:

1947. Maria Callas on the Rossija *cargo ship with colleague Nicola Rossi Lemeni and a Swiss friend.*

But this does not mean 'out of sight, out of mind.' I refuse to believe in this saying and I beg you not to believe in it either. Even if that is what others may tell you. Be satisfied with this. I believe that you are intelligent enough to understand more than I can write to you. . .

"Thanks to God, who has given me this angelic person. . . for the first time in my life I have no need of anyone else. I shall think deeply about the possibility of marrying him, I promise. But the truth is that it is so rare to find a kindred spirit. You know me well, my character, everything, and you must know that I am happy with him, he must be everything I desire. He is a little older than me, actually quite a bit older to tell the truth: He is fifty-two but looks after himself in every way. He also looks after me. He understands me perfectly and I understand him. After all, this is what counts most in life. Happiness and love, deeply felt love, are worth more than an awful career, which leaves nothing else except a name.

"For the first time, I have met my kind of man. Should I perhaps leave him and be unhappy for the rest of my life? He has everything I could ever want and adores me. That's it. It is not love, it is something more. You are intelligent and altruistic. Answer me.

"I am happy to have written this letter because it seems as if I have talked with you, as if you were here, close to me, much closer to me. Please, don't mind if I don't write to you very often. I am as bad as you are. Don't be an egoist and don't misunderstand me: I feel for you what I felt when I left you.

"I would like you to write back to me straightaway. Clearly and joyfully. Not as my manager, but as Eddie, my friend.

"Dearest, I am very tired after writing this long letter. Please try to read it all without becoming irritated and try to remember the good times we have had together, not the bad ones, as I try to do. I am always happy to have a person like you as a dear friend. Believe me, I love both of you, tirelessly. Kiss your family and our friends for me and shit to all those who are enemies to you and me.

"Anxiously waiting for your next letter and in the hope that you will always think of me as your Maria."

The date of this letter, August 20, coincided with another event involving Maria Callas: Meneghini's attempt to obtain from Serafin a recommendation for his protégé so that she could immediately embark upon a fine career.

Once the performances of *Gioconda* in the Arena were over, Meneghini, as he had promised, began to think of Maria's future. And the first thing he did was to talk to Serafin, who had conducted the singer in *Gioconda*. He would certainly have lent a hand, given her a recommendation, and made sure that she was taken on immediately at La Scala.

But Serafin was an extremely serious professional. He told Meneghini that Callas still had to study. It was too early in her career to risk a performance in the major opera theaters. "I can give you a letter of introduction to a singing teacher I know who will be able to advise your protégé," he said. They were talking at the Pedavena Restaurant, in Piazza Bra, in front of the Arena. Serafin asked the waiter to bring two sheets of paper and wrote the letter. Meneghini was angry. He didn't understand the conductor's prudence. He accepted the letter but he possibly never read it—a pity, since Serafin said wonderful things about Callas. He appears as the only one who

had completely recognized her artistic talent, in full, right from their first meeting.

He was a true connoisseur of voices. His every word was utterly well-measured. And reading this letter, we

Miss Kallas has a truly exceptional voice, which has all the scope to tackle even the most difficult parts. Strong, powerful notes and sweet and easy slow tones, a natural agility.

"She lacks only one thing: She

"I wanted to be in your arms, to feel you near to me as I have felt you before. You are so much mine and I thank you. I only ask for your love and affection."

perceive great and unconditional esteem. The letter was written to Mrs. Emma Molaioli.

"Dear lady Emma, the carrier of this letter is Miss Kallas, a young American singer who interpreted the character of Gioconda at the Arena with enormous success. As you will yourself realize,

needs to be made more Italian, in all her keys and all (illegible). She still lacks this because some of her vowels are not entirely Italian. Consequently, certain sounds are not entirely ours.

"I believe that only one person can help her achieve this balance: you, Mrs. Molaioli. Listen to her and tell Miss

Kallas and her companion, Mr. Meneghini, your full opinion. I am convinced that once this refinement, "nationalization" as we might say, is completed, we will have found the artist we have been looking for all these years.

"With Elena, Vittoria, Donatella, my sincerest best regards. Tullio Serafin."

As already said, Meneghini did not take Serafin's suggestion into consideration. He let things drop and even began to overlook Maria. He stopped writing her on August 14, the date of the last letter reprinted here. Maria, used to receiving his gallant letters almost every day, was upset. She could not understand the reason for this sudden change.

Meneghini had perhaps realized that nothing important was happening as regards her career. No invitations to sing had arrived. He probably thought that she had no real future. It was no longer good business for him. Perhaps,

in his heart, he thought he could send her back to America. Maria began to think less about matrimony. This appears clearly in a letter to Bagarozy written on September 2.

"My dearest Eddie, since I last wrote to you I have changed my mind. I have thought and thought and have finally reached the conclusion that I should not get married.

"It would be silly to marry him now, even if I do love him. I'm angry with myself, nevertheless: I have a rich and powerful man behinf me and I could sing where and when I wanted. I've had invitations from Barcelona, in Spain, to sing Norma and Forza del Destino. I think I should accept, don't you agree?

"Darling, what are you doing? I am happy for you. Keep on working and don't think that I have forgotten you. It is only circumstances that make us act

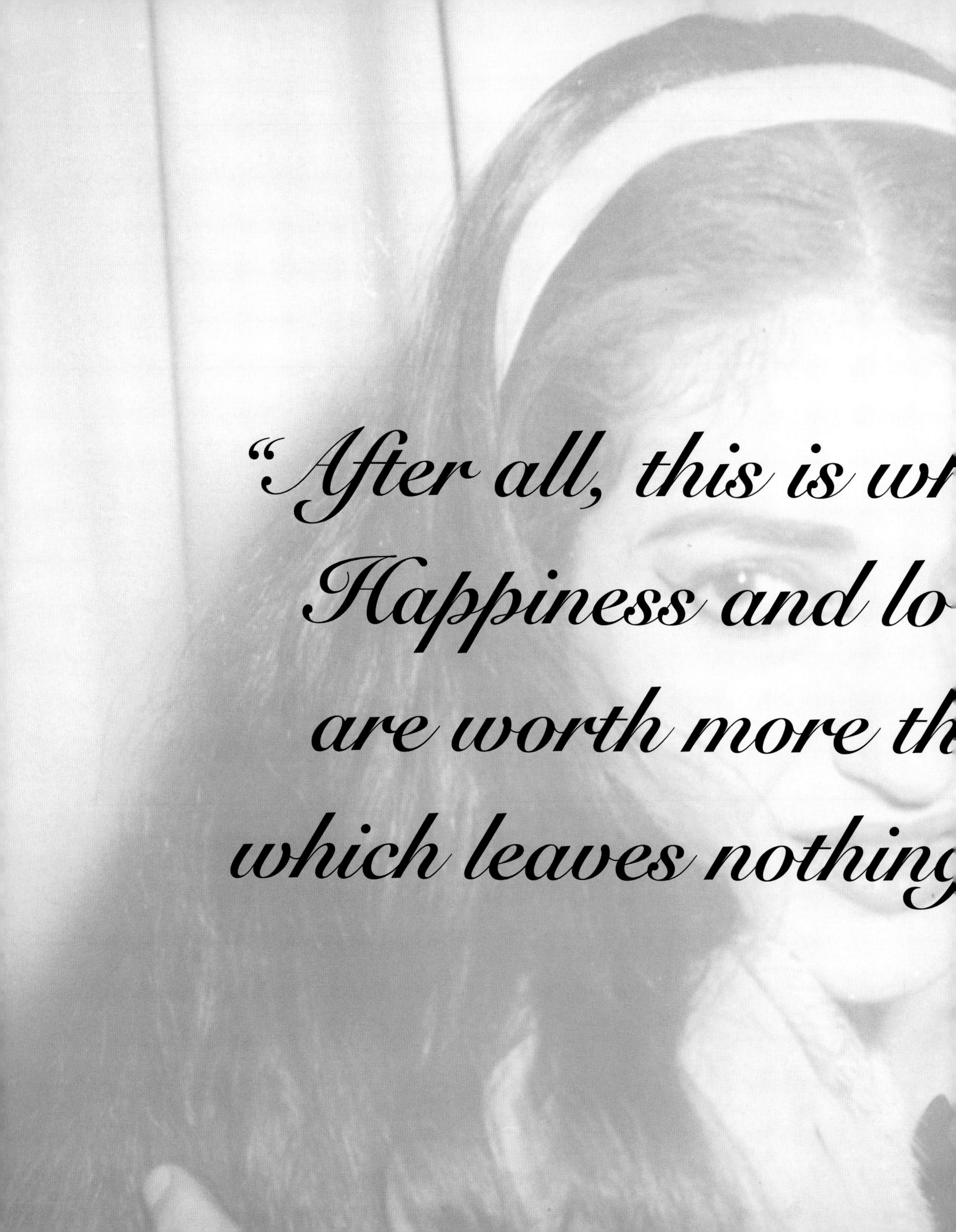

"After all, this is wh
Happiness and lo
are worth more th
which leaves nothing

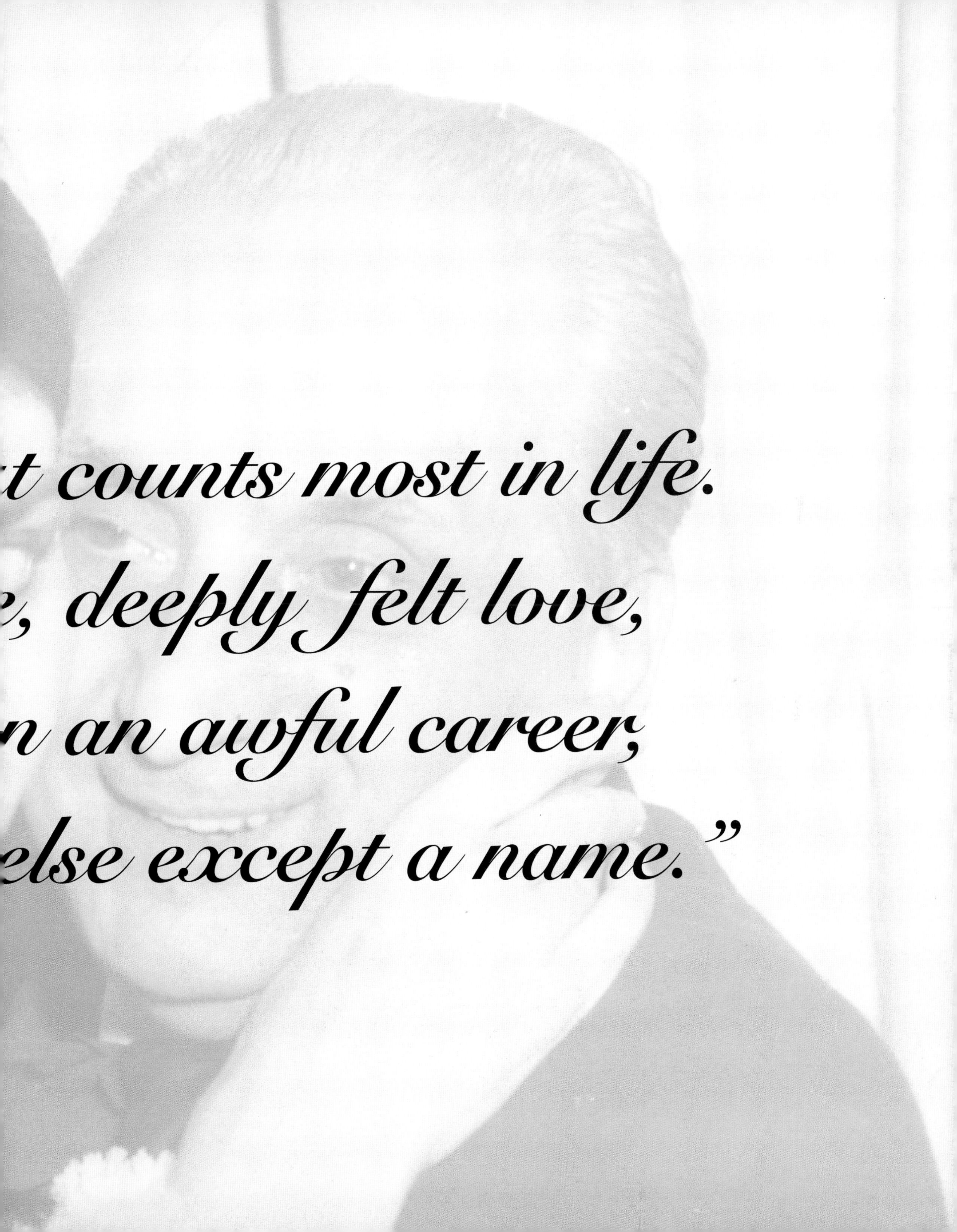

t counts most in life.

, deeply felt love,

n an awful career,

else except a name."

differently. When I see you, one day, I will explain everything!

"You should know one thing: Maria doesn't change as other people change. Even if you treated me very brusquely in the months before my departure, I said nothing and will continue to be faithful to you.

"Dearest, I must leave you now and wish you all the best. Please write back to me immediately and answer everything about my career and tell me if I'm doing the right thing. Forgive me the change in my character, but Battista does not like me to tell jokes. How I miss your jokes! Surely, I will also be an angel in heaven: Why ever not?

"Another favor, please: Don't go around gossiping about this and my other business and private affairs with our friends. I would not like that at all."

The crisis with Meneghini continued and became serious. Maria began to think about her future. What were her prospects? Pack her bags and return to America? First and foremost, her permit to stay in Italy was about to expire. She experienced hours of anxiety, made worse by Meneghini's behavior, which was cold and detached.

Suddenly, things changed. Meneghini went to see her in the hotel and was kind to her, staying to sleep as he had done before. Maria realized that he still cared about her, so she finally wrote her first letter to him, confiding her soul and her worries. She revealed to him that she had decided to pack her bags and go, but that now, after his demonstration of affection, had decided to change her mind and remain.

The letter is in Italian, in miniature, regular, and diligent handwriting.

Monday, September 22, 1947:

"My dearest Battista, Yesterday I tore up a letter I had written to you and am now writing another one. I hope it doesn't bore you.

"Battista, I feel that I have to tell you that my love for you is so strong and deep that at times it is even painful for me.

"The other night and all day yesterday were torture. Leaving you would have been too great a punishment and I don't think I would have managed it. Life could not give me a greater pain and I do not think I deserve it. I need you and your love.

"Yesterday, I had decided to leave because it seemed that you were bored with me the other evening. Yes, I was decided, but I had so many excuses not to make all the preparations, so many excuses not to leave in other ways, and so much hope that you would not want to see me leave, that I only packed half my baggage.

"If you were more shrewd you would have realized that I was waiting for nothing other than a gesture of yours, a word, to make me stay.

"You proved your love to me yesterday. I needed to feel and see that I am not a problem for you, that I do not bore you. I had suffered so much and was happy that you stayed with me like that. I would have felt so awful if you had left last night. I wanted to be in your arms, to feel you near to me as I have felt you before. You are so much mine and I thank you. I only ask for your love and affection.

"And I promise you that I will do my best to correct this big defect of mine. I only ask a little of your patience.

"So, today, thinking about everything, today I depend on your wishes. If you are tired of me, tell me and I will leave immediately. You ask my decision but today I no longer want to leave. I believe that I could not have left even yesterday. Yesterday I could not leave, today I don't want to!

"My Battista, you have everything of me, everything down to my deepest feelings, my smallest thought. I live for you. Your wishes are mine, I do everything you want, but please don't take this love and hide it away. I need your home. Every home has to be looked after. Don't forget that every woman thinks, lives, and depends on her man. For me, you are my man. No woman, Battista, could ever care more than I care for you.

"You have an obligation in your life now: to live and be well for me. Be especially well. Do your work, don't tire yourself and let me give you a little joy and satisfaction if I can, but only be mine.

"You have me and will always have me, remember this well. I became convinced yesterday that I cannot live without you. Dear, this is a very long letter and will perhaps annoy you. But I have to tell you these things.

"I am the friend of your heart, your confidant, your support when you are tired, everything I can do at any moment. I would like to be so much more but I don't know how. I shall try to be what you deserve. I would like to know if you want me to be always as before.

"Your Maria."

Life went on calmly. Meneghini decided to continue his interest in Maria. He began to contact other musicians to find her engagements. He obtained a recommendation from Maestro Antonio Guarnieri for an audition at La Scala. He telephoned several agencies. He arranged visits to Milan. He prepared the papers and documents to renew her permit to stay in Italy. Maria began to hope again.

The audition in Milan went badly. Maestro Mario Labroca, having heard Callas, said to Meneghini: "She's not worth anything. Send her back to America whenever you want. It'll be in your best interest."

Meneghini never told Callas about this assessment. He continued his efforts to find her a part. But even the agencies were unhopeful and replied negatively. The situation was difficult.

Maria, however, knew nothing of all this. She was convinced that her man could achieve anything and lived and did everything serenely, as this letter to lawyer Bagarozy written on October 25 demonstrates:

October 25:
"Ciao, my dear! You are sending me so many letters that I really do not know which one to read first. You skunk! And you even have the cheek to ask me to write to you. . .

"Isn't he a dear? Oh! He is full of these fine things, so dear. These are things I wanted which you did not understand. Dear, these things are never said, they are simply natural. The drama of the whole story is that he is so much older than me and I am stupidly young. Stupidly, because you know that I am much older in mind and character. . .

"Well, I shall end this letter with a kiss on both your cheeks. And . . . perhaps one on your sweet, tempting lips but I am frightened this would be untrue to Battista and too dangerous! So, no kiss on your lips but just one on your forehead. Ciao, and please, Eddie, try not to forget me."

"It would be silly to marry him now, even if I do love him.
I'm angry with myself, nevertheless:
I have a rich and powerful man behind me and
I could sing where and when I wanted.
I've had invitations
from Barcelona, in Spain, to sing Norma and Forza del Destino.
I think I should accept, don't you agree?

Opposite page, left:

1952. Maria Callas in the role of Elvira in Bellini's The Puritans.

Opposite page, below:

1947. Maria Callas in a photograph taken by her father George in New York shortly before her departure for Italy.

51

I Wa of

It was a foggy day on October 28, 1947. Maria Callas got up very early. Her companion, Giovan Battista Meneghini, took her to Verona station and Maria caught the train for Rome. She was going to study *Tristan and Isolde*, Wagner's opera, with the singing teacher recommended by Serafin. Callas was to take the leading female role at the Fenice Opera House in Venice.

This opera was to mark the beginning of her fabulous career. But she didn't know that. At that time, success was not at the center of her attention.

Maria was unhappy. By now she felt deeply in love with Meneghini, the man who had given her so much help since her arrival in Italy. Leaving him, for however short a time, pained her enormously. Her eyes were swollen; she had cried during the night. Close to despair, she looked out of the window, trying not to let the other passengers see

t the Best
e Best

her state of mind.

For two or three months, Callas, together with Meneghini, had tried to find an engagement in any theater simply so she could sing, but had only received refusals. *Gioconda*, which she had sung in the Arena in Verona in August, had not aroused any interest. Only Serafin, who conducted her in those performances, remembered her, and had searched her out to offer her the part of Isolde. Serafin was a highly renowned conductor and Maria should have been delighted to receive such an invitation. But so many disappointments had discouraged her. Her thoughts were turned to Meneghini. Despite everything, he was the only person who had ever really helped her. Without him, she may have returned to America and given up a singing career forever. Her love for Meneghini was by now sure and strong. But it was not an

overwhelming love, an irresistible passion; it was, instead, characterized by great tenderness and deep gratitude. Maria, however, had realized that Meneghini had changed somewhat over the last few weeks. He no longer displayed the enthusiasm and passion of their first meetings. But he was nevertheless always at her side and continued to take an interest in her problems.

On arrival in Rome, Maria Callas went immediately to Serafin's house. He suggested that she stay in a nearby hotel so she could easily study with him.

Maria was not in top physical form. Her leg, injured in the accident at the Arena, still hurt her. She could hardly carry her baggage. On reaching the hotel, she found it had no free rooms. She thus found herself on the street, with only her baggage in hand, to look for somewhere to stay. She realized that prices were rather high and that she should be careful with her expenses. Two months earlier, Meneghini would have made reservations, payments, and even arranged for flowers to be delivered to her room. Things were different now. Meneghini had not booked a room, nor had he given her very much money. She had to be frugal.

She toured several pensions to ask for prices. It was evening by the time she found somewhere to stay. She had walked all day long and was exhausted. The person destined to become a famous woman and an incomparable singer was badly dressed, pained, and alone in a room in a cheap hotel. "It is a pretty room," she wrote to Meneghini the next day, "small, a little damp (I hope I don't catch a cold) and unfortunately doesn't have its own bathroom. It costs around 1,100 lire. The other, newer pensions cost 3-4,000 lire a day. I think it is best for me to stay here because it is close to the bus stop to go to Serafin."

This simple, humble, and modest letter is a moving document, which captures the miserable conditions in which Callas found herself, and the consummate vastness of her heart. Despite her poverty, her difficulties, and her painful leg, she remained a sublime soul, uncontaminated by what happened around her.

"Dearest Battista, first of all I want to know how you are and if everything is going well. After, I want to tell you that I miss you very, very much. Last night was the first time I had a meal alone and I can't tell you how sad I felt. I wouldn't even bother to eat if it weren't necessary. Since I left you, I

she wanted to make him happy.

Love was critical to Callas in this period of her life. If it had been entirely up to her, she would have given up her career for a family life with the man she

without your news."

Maria stayed in Rome for one week and in that short time wrote nine letters to Meneghini. They are all full of immense love, her desire to return home, and the sadness she felt in being far away from him. They also reveal that her singing studies were going well, that Serafin was pleased, and that she intended to do her best to ensure a triumph. Not so much for her own future but because she had realized that this was very important to Meneghini. And

"I see that you are in love with Callas the artist. You forget my soul. For example, your letter was wonderful, so dear, but I wanted a little more Battista and Maria in it, not Meneghini and Callas. Let's see if I find my Battista in your next letters. . ."

have eaten nothing other than salads and eggs. I simply have no appetite. How shall I get by later if I already feel like this after only a few days apart? You are very busy, aren't you? What are you doing? My love, please don't leave me

loved. "Yes, my dear Battista, I will try to reach my goal because, above all, it will make you happy."

And she complains because Meneghini's letters were cold. "And me, who makes me happy? I make everyone

happy and all I am left with is glory, while my feelings count for nothing. . .

"Oh well, let's stop being philosophical because it makes me unhappy and sad. I see that you are in love with Callas the artist. You forget my soul. For example, your letter was wonderful, so dear, but I wanted a little more Battista and Maria in it, not Meneghini and Callas. Let's see if I find my Battista in your next letters. . .

"Today, my love, my leg hurt me a lot. It hurt so much at one point that I wanted to cry. I got on the bus, which has quite a high step, and the pain I felt was awful. For goodness sake, how much longer must I suffer this? Then I had a headache, one of those horrible

1951. Maria Callas, by now famous, wearing one of her extravagant hats. Recalling the elegance of the singer, fashion designer Biki said: "Callas had taste and was attracted to everything beautiful. She was a perfectionist: She personally selected the fabrics for her outfits. She sometimes even made suggestions, drawing pencil sketches on pieces of paper."

Center:

A close-up of Maria Callas's hands. The singer was also a talented pianist.

Below:

1948. Maria Callas with Giovan Battista Meneghini at the time of their wedding on April 21, 1949, at 4:00 p.m. in the sacristy of the Filippini Church in Verona, before the parish priest and two witnesses. Because Callas was Greek Orthodox, the bishop of Verona would not allow them to marry with a traditional ceremony, and he imposed a great many conditions. Immediately after the service, Meneghini accompanied Callas by car to the port of Genoa, where she boarded a ship for a three-month tour in South America.

ones which every now and then afflict me. I don't know what to say but when I am far from you I feel poorly. Battista, I miss you, you can't imagine how much."

On November 10, Maria returned to Verona and continued studying on her own. In the middle of December, she moved to Venice for stage rehearsals. *Tristan and Isolde*, staged on December 30, was a huge triumph. Everyone—the audience, the critics, the experts—finally recognized the exceptional artistry of Maria Callas. Serafin was enthusiastic. His wife, Elena Rakowska, who herself had been acclaimed for her portrayal of Isolde at the beginning of the century, repeatedly told her husband: "I told you

it would be a triumph."

Maria's spirits soared. It was her first real triumph. And, moreover, it was a total triumph. Inside, she thought of the rejection from La Scala. "We shall see if the management of La Scala gets in touch now," she repeated to Meneghini. She meditated on her words of revenge. But she did not yet fully fathom the mysterious gears behind the operations of the Milan Opera House, nor did she know how long she would have to wait before singing at La Scala.

Maria Callas stayed in Venice for two months. At the Fenice Opera House, she gave four performances in *Tristan and Isolde*, conducted by Serafin. She then took the leading role in Puccini's *Turandot*, conducted by Nino Sanzogno, for five nights, and her success was even more astonishing.

She now waited for the major theaters contact her, especially La Scala. The newspapers gave her ample coverage and she thought she had become the singer of the moment. But La Scala made no move. She began to realize that someone was blocking her way. She recalled the threatening telephone calls she had received after she won the part in *Tristan and Isolde*. Serafin received the same kind of call because he had given the part to a foreign singer. Articles attacking her began to appear in the United States.

The new year—1948—began well. Two marvelous triumphs at the Fenice in Venice and many newspaper articles were remarkable achievements. Since the major theaters hadn't contacted her, she decided to sing in the provinces. For the time being, she was only interested in singing.

She began a period of intense work. In March, Callas sang in Udine, where she had her first interviews. She wrote to Meneghini: "I was very tired. We arrived at 5 and the rehearsal began at 5:30 and went on until 8. Everyone was enthusiastic to hear me sing but I didn't use all my power because I thought it prudent not to force my voice. But, they were especially delighted with my marvelous pronunciation.

"In the evening, after dinner, the journalists came and asked questions about my life and career. They kept me up until after midnight. They complimented me on my good looks. In short, I received a very warm welcome.

"Later, yesterday, when I paid the bill for lunch, I almost fainted from sur-

prise. Just imagine: I had a risotto with butter, two eggs in butter, fennel and fruit salad, bread and coffee. It only came to 505 lire! I have never paid such a small bill. . .

"And what did you do yesterday and today? Did you eat, sleep, and work well? Did you think a little about me? I didn't lie to you on the phone. I am really not very well. Even as I spoke, I felt my heart break. You know how I feel when I am far away from you."

In April, she was in Trieste giving four performances of *Forza del Destino*. The welcome was very warm indeed. She wrote to Meneghini: "Franci says that no one in Italy sings Verdi as well

as I do. Towards evening, a journalist came for an interview. When I arrived at the hotel, I found that they had changed my room and this pleased me enormously. The new room is beautiful, large, with a spacious and lovely bathroom. I have just had a hot bath, and it was wonderful. My dear love, when will I see you? Battista mine, I am so unhappy away from you."

On the eve of her debut, the newspaper *Il Corriere di Trieste* published a long interview under the headline "Maria Callas didn't spend a penny to study singing." From Trieste, she went to Genoa, Rome, back to the Verona Arena, to Genoa again, and finally to Turin. At that time, the operas in her repertoire were *Tristan and Isolde, Turandot, Forza del Destino,* and *Aida*.

She worked hard and gained experience. She accepted engagements enthusiastically. Callas had found her ideal environment. She was calm in her private life because she was happily in love with Meneghini, and satisfied with her professional career because she was singing a great deal and every opera was a triumph. Her characterization later became more nuanced, more complex.

She transformed into her heroines with a facility and cohesion which startled everyone. Her voice was powerful and fresh. It was perhaps the best period in Maria Callas's career, not least because she was somewhat detached from her profession. She was mostly concerned about being in love.

She wrote a great deal to Meneghini from everywhere she went. In her letters, Callas mentioned the opera she was performing, made some remarks about her colleagues, the conductor, the audience, and then she let herself go—expressing her feelings for the man she loved. "My dear Battista, I cannot even try to explain how awful I felt when I heard you had left this morning. My God, Battista, what anxiety. . ."

"My dear love, when will I see you? Battista mine: I am so unhappy far from you. . . I'm writing these few lines because it makes me feel closer to you. Although you phoned yesterday, I feel so sad and alone. We were together so often recently, I was so used to being near you that I now feel tremendously empty. So, so empty. . ."

"It pleases me so much when you write to me. We can talk on the telephone, but time is short; it passes before I can begin to feel you with me. Letters are different. They stay with me, and I read and reread them. When I feel lonely, I take your letters and feel you closer to me. . ."

Maria always wrote long letters, at times very long. At certain times, when nostalgia was particularly strong, she wrote three or four times a day.

She rarely opened her letters in the same way: "Dear Battista," "My dear Battista," "My dear love," "My dear and adorable Battista," "My dearest soul," "Dear, Dear, Dear," "My adored and sublime love," "Dear, dearest, my reason for living," "My sweet Titta," "Dear, dear adored darling," "Mine," "Only you." Her signature was always the same:

Maria—written in a dry, regular, unchanging handwriting, like a stamp or trademark. But before her signature, the last few lines of farewell were consummately sweet and exceptionally varied. "I kiss you ardently and, dear, you do not know how much I desire you to madness. All of your Maria."

"I can only repeat I love you immensely and I respect and esteem you even more. I desire you infinitely, I am eternally your Maria."

"Write to me, eat, sleep and don't get angry, it's not worth the effort. You must look after yourself. I want you to be as strong as a bull. I adore everything, everything, everything about you, as always and more than ever. Maria."

"Dear, write to me and care about me, I would die without you, you who are love, faithfulness, nobility, refinement, all things in my ideals. Yours eternally, Maria."

"Write to me often, my dear, because it is the only thing that feeds me well. Every morning, as soon as I wake up, I read all your letters, as I also do before going to sleep. They comfort me. Even when I am sad, I take them up and read them and they give me so much courage. Ciao, my darling, care for me. My tenderness and love. Think of me always. Your Maria."

"I adore you. Remember it, and that disappointment on your part would break my heart forever. I want you to know this. Ciao, my soul. Always your Maria."

"So many infinite tendernesses, together with all the kisses and caresses eternally yours from Maria."

"But I care for you and esteem you so highly that it seems I could never give you nor tell you enough. If I could offer my life itself for you, to prove how much I adore you, I would do so willingly. Dearest, I leave you now but I'm not really leaving you because I am with you, and can't say I'm going. So I kiss

"The horrible and boring news is that I have to wear a wig for Norma. I have to become a reddish blonde: How awful. It means I have to wear a wig. I will also have a kind of bustier exposing my waist. On top of this, the dress will be rather transparent and I will have to wear light stockings, not dark as for Aida. Poor me and poor you, who will have to see me dolled up like this. . ."

57

you so much to give you my all and disappear in you. Write to me, write to me, don't let even one day go by without sending me your news. Yours until death, Maria."

In October 1948, while singing *Aida* in Turin, Maria was introduced by Serafin to Francesco Siciliani, an art director in Florence. He was an ingenious musician, and the recently appointed art director of the Florentine May Music Festival (he had the same role at San Carlo in Naples for eight years). Rather shy and reserved, he did not particularly stand out, although his training and culture were of a much higher level than all other Italian musical directors.

Siciliani had not met Maria before. He agreed to listen to her only because she was introduced by Serafin. But, after only the first few notes, he grasped her exceptional artistic gifts. Convinced of her excellence and rare vocal dexterity, he asked her to debut in *Norma*, Bellini's masterpiece, due to be staged at the Comunale Theater in Florence at the end of the year. If Tullio Serafin was the first orchestra conductor to recognize Maria Callas's greatness, Siciliani was

would be a milestone in her career. She prepared intensely for it. She mentioned *Norma* in all her letters to Meneghini at this time.

"I have never seen Maestro so happy. I'm not so happy because I ask too much of myself. Believe me, it would be better if I had more time because one can never study *Norma* too much."

She was rather worried about the costumes and the wig. "The horrible and boring news is that I have to wear a wig for *Norma*. I have to become a reddish blonde: How awful. It means I have to wear a wig. I will also have a kind of bustier exposing my waist. On top of this, the dress will be rather transparent and I will have to wear light stockings, not dark as for Aida. Poor me and poor you, who will have to see me dolled up like this. . .

"I had to look around a lot to find the wig but at last I found one. You have to be careful with red. It can irritate the eyes. I chose something halfway between chestnut blonde and Titian red. I found a very lovely one, although it took a lot of effort. What's more, the wig must be very long, at least down to the

by this ocean of passion. But her voice did not always obey her intentions. It was a dramatic moment which involved not only her interpretative conscience but also her entire life. In the attempt to reach, to grasp the infinite beauty she sensed in *Norma*, she experienced, profoundly, the despair of the human predicament. But she refused to give in and reacted violently, like Prometheus, aiming always for perfection.

On November 18 she wrote an astonishing letter. Maria spoke of her art, expressed her thoughts, her ideals, her uncertainties, her worries, and her fears in facing the task for which she was preparing. It is an extraordinary document, and helps us understand how she worked inside herself to become the great artist later acclaimed universally.

"Dear, I was studying *Norma* after returning from rehearsals with the mezzo-soprano and you couldn't imagine how melancholy I became. So much so that I have to write to you to feel that I am a little closer to you and get things off my chest.

"You see, dear, I am such a pessimist and everything afflicts and disturbs me. I am convinced that I do everything badly. Then I begin to get nervous and discouraged. At times, I reach the point of begging to die to be freed of the torments and anxieties that always afflict me.

"You see, I would like to give so much more in everything I do. In art as in my love for you. In singing, I would like my voice always to do what I want. Yet it seems I ask too much. My voice is ungrateful and doesn't come out as I want. On the contrary, I would even say that it is rebellious and will not be commanded or, rather, dominated. It always wants to escape and makes me suffer. If I carry on like this, you will have a nervous breakdown on your hands. It is like this even in my love for you. I suffer because I don't know how to give you more. I would like, I don't know how, always to offer more and more. I know that I have no more to give you because I am only a human being, but I would like to be able to do so.

"Art, in the opinion of others, should be entirely for me. In my opinion it is not even the smallest part of what I would like it to be. Audiences applaud me, but I know, inside myself, that I could have achieved so much more. Serafin says that he is highly delighted

". . . I want the best of the best. I want my man to be the best of all. I want my art to be the most perfect. I want, in short, to have the best of everything. Even my clothes: I want them to be the best possible to be had. I know that all this is not possible and it torments me greatly. Why?"

the first artistic director to exploit her talents intelligently. He offered her operas which were particularly well-suited to highlighting her extraordinary interpretative ability. It was Siciliani who, after *Norma*, offered her *La Traviata*, *Lucia di Lammermoor* and *Armida* by Rossini, the latter never being performed because there were no singers capable of interpreting it. Siciliani also arranged for a role in Cherubini's famous *Medea*, which was one of the most memorable triumphs at La Scala. These were all operas in which Callas's excellence knew no rivals.

While in Rome at Serafin's home studying *Norma* for the Comunale in Florence, Maria realized that this opera

middle of my waist. Since I am very tall, and, bearing in mind that the wavy style will make the wig shorter, I need one at least 35″ long. Frankly, I was lucky to find one this long. Now I am happy, but at last I can concentrate on my voice."

Callas had understood that to interpret the priestliness and drama of Norma she needed a special voice. Bellini had created great melodies for his heroine, full of passion and infinite sadness. As she continued studying the opera, Callas knew that she could penetrate the heart of the character. She felt like Norma. Measuring up continually, repeatedly, to the immortal music of the young Bellini, she constructed the imposing heroine inside her, and matured with her. She felt overwhelmed

with my Norma. But, unfortunately, I am not in the least content. I am convinced I can do one hundred times better. But my voice doesn't respond and doesn't give what I expect.

"My love, why should I be made like this? I think I am the only person with such a discontented temperament. The only time when I do not want anything more than what I already have is when I am where I belong, when I am near you. I understand that daily necessities force us to be apart at times, but I am not the kind of person to take things as they come. I want the best of the best. I want my man to be the best of all. I want my art to be the most perfect. I want, in short, to have the best of everything. Even my clothes: I want them to be the best possible to be had. I know that all this is not possible and it torments me greatly. Why? Help me Battista, don't think I'm exaggerating,

it's the way I am."

The performance of *Norma* was a triumphal success. The part of Adalgise alongside Maria was sung by Fedora

Above:

1950. A view of the Palacio de Bellas Artes Theater in Mexico City where Callas performed four operas between May and June with enormous success.

Side:

1949. Maria Callas with Matilde, the housekeeper in the home in Verona where Callas went to live after marrying Meneghini.

Barbieri, a famous mezzo-soprano who took the stage with Callas in almost all the operas of her early career. The critics praised Callas unconditionally. Virgilio

wrote in *La Nazione*: "Maria Callas was a new name for us, but even after her opening in the first act we immediately realized that we were listening to a

On December 5, Maria gave her last performance of *Norma* in Florence and returned to Verona. The day after, she felt unwell. She thought it was the stress, but had severe abdominal pains in the evening of December 7. The doctor sent her to the hospital. It was appendicitis, requiring an operation. She remained in the hospital until December 18.

She spent Christmas in her own home in Verona and then left for Venice where she took Wagner's leading *Valkyrie* role, conducted by Serafin. It was in Venice that she achieved new heights, this time of a technical nature, which were to become legendary. While she sang Brunhilde in *Valkyrie*, she also took the role of Elvira in Bellini's *The Puritans*.

"Everyone was enthusiastic to hear me sing but

I didn't use all my power because I thought it prudent not to force

my voice. But, they were especially delighted with

my marvelous pronunciation."

Doplicher wrote in *Nuovo Corriere*: "...This young artist has already attained the highest levels of Italian *bel canto*, fine singing." Gualtiero Frangini

soprano of truly magnificent gifts."

Siciliani was very pleased with the results and immediately booked Callas for the following season.

These roles, from a vocal and technical point of view, are worlds apart. The first requires the voice of a dramatic soprano, the second a lighter, coloring soprano. No singer is able to tackle these two roles in rapid succession without running the risk of ruining her voice forever. Only Maria Callas has ever achieved this feat, demonstrating that she could, thanks to her voice and technique, cover any repertoire.

Immediately after *Valkyrie*, the Fenice program had scheduled Bellini's *The Puritans,* an extraordinary opera which is rarely performed for a lack of suitable singers. One of the singers of the time who was able to tackle this role was Margherita Carosio, a lyric soprano of great agility at the peak of her career. The performance of "*The Puritans*" at the Fenice Opera House had been arranged especially for her. But ten days before going onstage, Margherita Carosio was taken ill. The management desperately sought a stand-in, but it was impossible to find anyone up to the undertaking. It was Serafin's wife, Elena Rakowska, who suggested: "Only Callas can handle this opera." Serafin replied: "It's absurd. Maria is performing a demanding role in *Valkyrie* with a completely different musical texture than that of *The Puritans*. It is impossible to think she could sing in the two operas simultaneously. Moreover, there is no time to prepare the opera." "Maria can do it," retorted Elena Rakowska. And in the end, Serafin decided to risk the adventure because there were no other solutions.

Serafin called Callas and outlined the problem. Maria did not know *The Puritans*. She asked for the score and took a day to study it. The morning after, she said, "It's possible."

There were only eight days left before the premiere. In that brief space of time Maria had to complete three performances of *Valkyrie* and learn the new

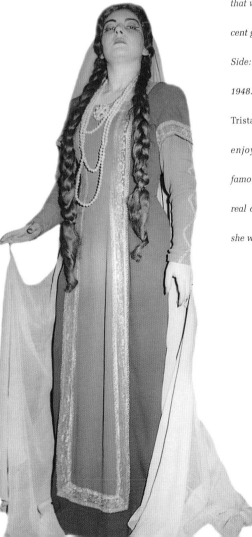

opera. She followed the program to the letter. On the first night, the theater was full to overflowing. The audience was mostly composed of admirers of Margherita Carosio, coming from all over to applaud their favorite. As a result, they were not very welldisposed towards the young Callas. The performance risked turning out to be a disaster. Instead, it was a triumph of a kind rarely ever seen. The audience was moved to tears and the fans of Margherita Carosio were the most fanatical in their applause. Critic Vardenega wrote the following day: "The surprise was that Callas proved to be an incomparable Elvira. From her demanding role as Brunhilde, she became an agile and sensitive creature, alive in every note, her singing full of higher intelligence." Mario Nordi: "A few days ago, many were taken aback to read the name of a magnificent Brunhilde, Isolde, and Turandot announced in the role of

Elvira. Last night, everyone heard her and even the most skeptical had to admit that Maria Callas achieved a miracle."

Maria enjoyed continual triumphs. She had become famous and earned a great deal of money but her real dream was her home. If it had been up to her, she would have given up her career to be a wife. She wanted to marry Meneghini.

There had been talk of marrying for some time but there were various difficulties. Meneghini's brothers hated her and did everything to persuade him to leave her. They even reached the point of pushing her down stairs. Another difficulty was that Maria did not have the necessary documents with her. Additionally, she was Greek Orthodox.

One morning, towards the end of March, she said to Meneghini "If you don't marry me I won't sing again." She knew that Meneghini was very interested in the substantial fees that she was being offered by now and this struck home. Meneghini, on his part, by now knew her well enough to know her

words were serious: She really would have been capable of turning her threat into reality. He had no choice but to condescend.

Maria dreamed that her wedding day would be splendid, a marvelous celebration, full of happiness, a white

Catholics to marry anyone of Orthodox origins.

Meneghini had to resort to all his influential friendships. In the end, he even went to the bishop, threatening a huge scandal if the procedures were not terminated quickly. The bishop gave in

"I want to tell you something odd: Every morning at 6:30 or 7, I suddenly open my eyes with the sensation that somebody has come to wake me up. I think it is you and I am happy. . ."

gown, plenty of guests, a flower-decked church, and the sound of an organ playing. Meneghini began to take steps to organize the event but as he went on he realized that things were complicated. The difficulties even seemed insurmountable—not the least because Maria belonged to the Orthodox Church. At that time, Catholics treated Orthodox believers like infidels. The Catholic Church itself made it very difficult for

but the couple had to accept a whole number of humiliating conditions. The curia established that they could not marry with a solemn ritual, that the ceremony had to be held almost in secret and without guests to avoid creating too much fuss. The wedding ritual could not be held inside the church itself because Maria was not a Catholic; it could only take place in the sacristy.

The wedding of the most famous

"God who is good and gre

Because I have

However, I have u

has given me my revenge.

ever hurt anyone.

rked very hard. . ."

singer of the century was therefore very much a third-class and largely clandestine affair, as if it were not a celebration but a reproval, something of which to be ashamed. The wedding took place on April 21 at 4:00 p.m. in the Filippini Church. In truth, it was a room next to the sacristy used to store chairs, old headless statues, funeral drapes, baldachins, and banners. Two candles

were lit; there were no flowers and no other decoration. The couple were only accompanied by two witnesses, the sacristan, and the parish priest who performed the wedding ceremony. Immediately after the wedding, Meneghini jumped in the car and took Maria to the port of Genoa, where she sailed for a tour of South America.

The departure for South America on the ship *Argentina* was set for midnight. On the quayside in Genoa, Maria gave her brand-new husband a very emotional farewell. She was due to embark for Buenos Aires and would have been away for three months.

Up until the last minute, Maria did everything possible to avoid leaving. A few minutes before going on board, she said to her husband: "Let's ask Serafin if he can replace me." Meneghini went to speak with Serafin but the answer was negative. "The whole tour," said Serafin, "is hinged precisely on Maria's reputation." At midnight, the ship's horns rang out and it began to move.

The cast on that tour included Mario Del Monaco, Fedora Barbieri, Nicola Rossi Lemeni, and Mario

Filippeschi. Almost all of them travelled with close companions. Serafin even had his whole family with him. Maria was completely alone. It was the first long trip she had made since meeting Meneghini.

She tolerated her solitude for the first few days, but was then overwhelmed with sadness, which she released in the continuous letters she wrote to her husband.

It is interesting to relive that tour through Maria's letters: They are a kind of diary of her thoughts and feelings. They show that singing and music were extremely important to her, but not her highest aspirations in life. She speaks little of her performances in these letters, but complains continually of having to be away from her husband. She

was famous by now and would have had many good reasons for thinking of her career and glory, yet, had it been up to her, she would have abandoned everything and returned home.

April 22:
"My dear Battista, just a few lines of greeting from Barcelona. I think of you more than ever in these days which should rightly be ours together. As I told you a few days ago, I left in much happier spirits. This trip will perhaps be less painful than the others since we met because the happiness in belonging completely to you gives me comfort in an indescribable way. . .

"Make sure you eat, sleep. . . You are mine and I am yours. . . I will keep well (with God's help) for you, I shall sing and be famous for you. You must look after yourself for me. . . I have placed our little Madonna over my bed. . . The weather is good and I shall try to exercise to lose some weight."

April 26:
"Dear, dear, dear, I have only been sailing for four days but I already miss you terribly, I have no words to describe how bored I am and pray to God that this trip will be over as soon as possible so that I can return to you. . .

"I want to tell you something odd: Every morning at 6:30 or 7, I suddenly open my eyes with the sensation that somebody has come to wake me up. I think it is you and I am happy. . .

"It seems that they want to play a bad trick on me at the Colon in Buenos

Aires, but they shall pay for it! They are thinking of opening with *Aida* but not with me singing. It seems that a certain Minkus will sing. . .

"Dear, I adore you much more than you could believe. You are my man in front of God and all men and I am proud of you and ask nothing more of life than to make you happy. . . Think of me as I think of you and care for me a quarter of how much I care for you."

May 6:
"If it is true that souls can speak to each other even when far apart, you will have been woken up by my shouts. I was desperate. There was a film at the cinema which was horrible; it was a war film, with torture and destruction, and you know how easily moved I am. I

67

burst into tears and could not calm myself down. I called for you so many times. I tried to remember the words you whisper to calm me. But it was even worse. Thinking of you made me feel even more unhappy. . .

"The other day there was a masked ball on board and I was so beautiful that you would have fallen in love with me again. Elena Rakowska had the idea of dressing me in an ancient Greek costume. I simply wrapped a sheet around myself and wore my hair high as they did in ancient Greece. Can you imagine, I won the prize for the most original costume. They took a photograph of me, which I enclose."

May 13:
"I was unable to continue writing this letter the other day because I really did feel unwell. So unwell that I went straight to bed and remained there until today. Three days in bed: Just think how angry and sad I was. I damn the day I left and I am furious because you allowed me to leave. I can't live

without you: It's time you understood that. . .

"The management of the Rio Theater have told me they would like to stage *Norma* with me. I refused because I said I had to return to Italy. Now, if you really want me to return to you, you must help me. You must write immediately to Serafin saying that you absolutely want me back in Italy as soon as possible, otherwise you won't allow me to sing next winter. Or else invent something else of this kind. Write to me as well so that I can show Serafin the letter. You must do this immediately

because Montevideo also wants me. You must say that you only allowed me to leave for Argentina provided that I returned as soon as possible without taking on any other engagements. . ."

"It seems that God has heard my prayers because everyone at the rehearsals yesterday were left speechless with enthusiasm. Scatto was there, poor man, jumping for joy. He said "This is singing, this is how singing used to be". . ."

May 14:
"Dear, is it possible for my love to grow? It seemed to me that I had given you everything but I understand that your every word, your every gesture of tenderness increases the paradisaical love I feel for you. . .

"You do everything I desire before I even ask it of you. . . I thank you deeply for having agreed to marry me before leaving. You made my love for you even bigger this way. Our love must always be seen as a symbol by the rest of the world. . . I forgot to tell you that I deliberately left my lovely pink nightdress in the wardrobe. I left it for you. It belongs exclusively to you. I shall only ever wear it for you. I shall wear it on the first night after I return. Are you thinking about that night?!!! We shall both explode with love and tenderness. I shall come back by aeroplane because I do not want to waste another twenty days on ship. I would certainly go crazy. If you intend to come here, I don't want you to fly. It's not important if anything happens to me. But I could not stand it if anything happened to you. If we have to die, better to die together."

May 15:
"Buenos Aires is beautiful, huge, and full of enormous cars, the ones you call homes. There are fine shops and spacious streets but my heart is over there with you. And here I do not see nor enjoy any beauty. You are my reason for living. I adore you so much that I want to die in your arms."

May 16:
". . . I called Covies, the lady who wrote to me from here, do you remember? I agreed to let her help me a little. I will give her something every month and she will look after my wardrobe. Her daughter will be my secretary. They don't want anything but they are poor and I will help them. . . The coffee here is awful. From what I see around, elegance is disappointing. It's better in Italy where people are more courteous and life is more lovely. . . Write to me my dear because your letters are the only thing that keep me alive."

May 17:
". . . This small apartment suits me. I have a small kitchen which is very use-ful. I've just gone to take some milk off the gas. I shall now drink a warm glass with plenty of sugar and plenty of cognac to try and get rid of this bothersome cold. . . This morning, I woke up around 7 with a strange headache. I thought I had a tumor, honestly. It hurt even to the touch. I had to get up and take two aspirins. . . Please write to Serafin telling him to send me home as soon as possible. Remind him that we have just got married and that you have every right for me to be with you. Move him, because he is old and, perhaps, after many years of marriage doesn't remember the joy of two newlyweds in love like us."

May 26:

"Mine, I was awoken this morning by the maid bringing me your letter. It was the best awakening I have ever had. . .

"Tomorrow is the first night of *Aida* and I'm rather upset. Rigal will sing and will also take *Forza del Destino*. I'm not much bothered about *Forza* but I am about *Aida*. Serafin says he might convince Grassi-Diaz to give me two performances. For comparison. . ."

May 27:

". . . The flu has helped me lose weight. I am a little drawn in the face. If you were to see me, you'd be furious. I am skinny and, as you would say, 'pale and down at heel.' Even Rossi has said I look drawn. . . I am not jealous, because no other woman would be able to love you the way I do. Nor give you the satisfaction I have given and will always give you. . .

"*Aida* is on tonight with Rigal. You can imagine how I feel. I swear to you that I haven't felt so bad for ages. Perhaps since I sang *Tristan* in Venice. I'm suffering tremendously. I feel that my whole body hurts and there is so much pain in my heart. Here, everyone is interested only in themselves. When I was unwell, only Maestro came to see me, risking catching the flu himself. . .

"It is a fine day outside, it seems like spring. But it would be more of a bother than a pleasure to go out. The weather changes from one moment to the next. It is hot and then it is cold. It is very humid and my leg hurts. It's disastrous."

May 30:

". . . And then I'm annoyed with you. It's not fair that you only write every three days and then only a few lines. I hate writing but I write a lot and often to you. Knowing that I live waiting for your letters, you should send me more of them. . ."

June 6:

". . . It's Friday and there was no mail and I feel alone and abandoned. When I come back, you must give me more caresses than you could ever imagine. I cannot and will never be able to explain how much I have suffered recently."

June 8:

"At last, your mail has come. Six letters all in one go. *Norma* will be staged on the 17th, eight days from now. You see, people cannot appreciate my art in *Turandot*. My colleagues haven't had

Opposite page:

1955. Maria Callas embraced affectionately by

orchestra conductor Leonard Bernstein at the end of

the first night of Sonnambula at La Scala.

Side:

Maria Callas with her husband, Meneghini, and her

father, George, in New York.

the fortune to sing with me. But with that horrible Rigal. They now have such grand airs about themselves. Especially that idiot Rossi, who has become quite insufferable to me. I will explain why when I get home. If I ever have the chance to prevent anything important for him, I shall do so willingly. Even if I am not the kind who enjoys that kind of thing. . .

"While I was ill, none of my colleagues came to see me. They were all happy because I was not singing. They

itself applauded. The people were taken aback. There's something funny in the air! Every now and then, the gossip is that I'm ill and they will have to change the performance. It always happens when I have a good rehearsal. It seems I bother some people a lot. Let them say what they want. The important thing is that you keep well. They shall see, later. I like to provoke people."

June 17:
"My dearest Battista, I am going to write

"Dear Battista, I have to make a confession. I would dearly like to have a child, our child. I think it would even be good for my voice and my terrible skin. . ."

are all afraid, poor things. They know they pale to nothing next to me. . .

"I can't wait to be in your arms again and live and flower again. Because you know how to give me all the satisfactions I want and help me forget everything."

June 12:
". . . I've had plenty to do to get my voice back in shape. Singing every twelve days is no good. . .

"I am so disgusted with the awful way my colleagues behave. I anxiously wait to find refuge in our pure and clean and dignified love. . .

"Yesterday, we had the first rehearsal with the orchestra, with Barbieri, Acts Two and Three. Everyone was astonished. After the duets, the orchestra

to you today, the day of the great test, of the great lesson in singing I intend to give everyone. The dress rehearsal was staged yesterday. . . It astonished everyone. Everyone was in tears over *Casta diva.* . .

"The other day, I went with a Greek journalist and a lady of the Greek Orthodox Church to light a candle for us and my *Norma.* You see, I feel my church more than I feel yours. Perhaps because I am used to it and perhaps because it is warmer and more lively. It's not that I don't like yours, which is mine, too, now, but I have a weakness for the Orthodox Church. . .

"It seems that God has listened to me since those who were at the rehearsal yesterday truly did not know what to say in their enthusiasm. There was Scatto, poor thing, who could hardly

contain himself. He said: "This is singing, this is how singing used to be. . ." Grassi-Diaz came up to me and embraced and kissed me, saying, "I am so enthusiastic and I must show it. Today, I cried." I heard that the choir wants to give me a gift, they were so pleased with me. Poor things. God who is good and great has given me my revenge. And this is because I have never hurt anyone. Because I have worked so hard. . .

"My love, in a month, if God wishes, we will see each other again and we shall always be together. Loving each other. Because this is the great thing of our love: We each give to the other. And the more one gives, the more the other gives, too. This is the love I have always dreamed and thought about. Now I have it. And I will care for it more than my own eyes."

June 20:
". . . As you will have understood, I have been up against a lot here. When I arrived, the place was hostile. Not only Grassi-Diaz, but all the others. I thus had to give them a little lesson of my superiority and worth by singing well. And I sang well. I brought the house down. No one had ever seen such success, not even Muzio. Now, they cannot say a thing. They've had to swallow their pride over everything they said about me, horrible people. And now, if God helps me, I shall give them another lesson with *Aida*. And then I shall return home and find comfort, peace, and love in your arms, my only aspiration. My dear, I missed you the other night. You would have cried for the emotion of such a triumph. I cried because you weren't here. . .

"Buenos Aires is quite hateful to me. The climate is awful. Too much smog everywhere. And then it is very fascist. All the fascists of the universe are here. Even the theater is under the control of Evita."

June 22:
"My dear adored one, I send you the local newspapers. They write marvelously well."

June 24:
"My adored and sublime love, today, the day of Saint John the Baptist, is your name day. . . The Serafins send their best regards, they speak often of you and I feel myself explode with happiness and pride. . . Serafin made me. You

know how he studies with me, don't you? You heard *Parsifal* at his house in Rome? He gives me his soul because, musically speaking, I respond to him to perfection. He also suffered when he saw how the people here were hostile towards me. Yesterday, Rigal gave her last performance of *Aida* and had the bad luck to strike a really awfully off-key right in 'Cieli azzurri', where she usually gives her best note, since she doesn't have many others. This happened precisely on her final night just as I am about to take her place. You see, dear, God is great. You only have to know how to wait and avoid hurting anyone to find justice."

July 3:
". . . By now I am so taken with the idea of returning that letters seem pointless to me. This one may even arrive with me. . . You will find me perhaps a little fatter: I was feeling so poorly that I ate like a horse to get back on my feet. So, if you don't want to see me look like Caniglia, you must help me eat little and only grilled meat and raw vegetables. You'll be in trouble if you don't help me. . .

"So, yesterday I sang *Aida*, at last. It was a triumph. I got back the respect I deserve from everyone. . . I also had the luck to please the minister. For the concert to celebrate Independence Day on July 9, I will sing *Norma* almost entirely alone. The minister asked that the duet with Adalgise and Pollione be cut because the tenor is awful. Rigal won't sing because Evita doesn't want her to. I am lucky, right? God always rewards the just. . . I won't write any more beautiful words because I will be able to tell you everything in person in eleven days time."

As we can see from these excerpts, Maria Callas—touring for one of the most important tests in her career—thought always and continuously of her husband. For her, professional interests always came after her private life. This was how Callas was and always remained.

She returned to Italy on July 14, 1949. Meneghini went to meet her at Rome Airport and accompanied her to Venice for a short holiday.

On returning to Verona, they began to furnish their new home. It was the first real home Maria ever had. She took on a housekeeper, named Matilde, with whom she continually moved furniture around to improve the appearance of the various rooms. She even bought a metal

Opposite page:

1951. Maria Callas, by now established as the queen

of La Scala, surprised by photographers with the

score in one hand as she was going to the theater

for rehearsals. Callas sang for the first time at La

Scala in April 1950 but her appearances went

entirely unnoticed, largely because of the hostility

towards her on the part of Antonio Ghiringhelli,

superintendent of the theater. Maria's first true sea-

son at La Scala began in December 1951, when she

made a triumphal entrance into the Milan theater

thanks to support from Arturo Toscanini.

Side, top:

1951. Maria Callas, middle, in the role of Eurydice,

during an interval in Haydn's opera Orpheus and

Eurydice at the Teatro della Pergola, Florence, con-

ducted by Eric Kleiber.

Side, bottom:

1953. Maria Callas with Fedora Barbieri in

Cherubini's Medea, the opera which opened that

year's May Music Festival in Florence. It was in this

period that she lost a great deal of weight, a topic

gossiped about in newspapers all over the world.

toolbox, like the ones plumbers and electricians use, and attached a note to it saying: "This toolbox must always be kept tidy and in good working order." Inside, there was everything needed for little jobs around the house: hammer, tongs, nails, screws, pliers, screwdriver, and various tools. She always kept it by her side, like a travel bag. Meneghini was a collector of antique pictures and Maria spent hours repairing them and changing their positions with Matilde's help. She was truly in love with her home.

She had a dream: to have a child. It has been written that Callas never wanted children so as not to interfere with her career, and that Meneghini did not want children either. A biographer wrote: "One day, in 1957, Maria Callas told her husband she wanted a child; but, Meneghini refused, saying that a child would have prevented her from looking after her career and ruined her chances for certain success."

These are fantasies and inventions. From the beginning of their marriage, Callas and Meneghini tried to have a child, as Maria's letters clearly prove. Every month she complained that she was not pregnant. In one letter, she wrote: "Dear Battista, I have to make a confession. I would dearly like to have a child, our child. I think it would even be good for my voice and my terrible skin. . ."

From Naples, in December 1949, where she was performing *Nabucco*, she wrote: "My dear, I am at a table in a restaurant trying to have a bite to eat before this evening's performance. I have received telegrams from all over

the universe. Naturally, I would have preferred you to be here, but let's be patient. I am well, in any case, and thank God. Let's hope everything goes as I would like. We really needed more rehearsals. I don't know what to do here. Going to the cinema on my own annoys me because I am worried about hangers-on. The weather is like spring outside, it is truly enchanting.

"I have to tell you that we won't be having a child this time either. I was regular again on the 18th, with a headache worthy of our worst enemies. We shall have to be patient."

The "Ca at La

On her return from the long tour in South America, Maria Callas commenced an intense performance schedule in Italy. On September 18 she sang in Perugia; in early November, she went to Turin to record *Tristan and Isolde*, *Norma*, and *The Puritans* for Cetra. In December, she moved to Naples to inaugurate the San Carlo Theater season with *Nabucco*.

In the beginning of 1950 she performed *Norma* in Venice, then *Aida* in Brescia. At the same time, she sang *Tristan and Isolde* at the opera theater in Rome and was forced to travel back and forth between the cities. Having finished the performances of *Aida* in Brescia, she moved definitively to Rome to sing in *Aida* and *Norma*.

She was working busily and determinedly. "I am a passionate artist and a passionate human being," she later stated, describing herself. "I become impatient when I'm held to the usual standards of work. I believe in self-discipline and self-control. If you want to live in harmony with yourself, you have to work. Work very hard. I don't agree with Descartes: "I think therefore I am." My motto is "I work therefore I am."

Callas was a Stakhanovite when it came to music. And everyone who ever worked with her agrees, saying that she was the first to arrive at rehearsals and the last to go. "A professional of

admirable seriousness and intransigence," commented Maestro Carlo Maria Giulini, who conducted her in some unforgettable masterpieces. "She wanted perfection in everything, even the smallest details."

She was immensely gratified by all this hard work. Audiences applauded and almost all the critics praised her, but she always had a cross to bear in her heart: to be able to sing at La Scala in Milan—an achievement which she always felt was beyond her reach.

La Scala has always been the most prestigious opera house in the world. It is considered a "temple" of opera, which every singer hopes to conquer. Maria also had an account to settle with the Milan theater: In September 1947, the management had rejected her. She wanted her revenge.

The leading prima donnas sang at La Scala, including some young singers such as Renata Tebaldi. And Maria couldn't help wondering why she was never invited. She racked her brains to find the best approach. She tried more than once to get in touch with Antonio Ghiringhelli, the superintendent of the theater, but as soon as he heard her name Ghiringhelli made sure he was unavailable. Maria also knew that, on various occasions, Ghiringhelli had objected, blatantly, to her singing at La Scala.

In February 1950, La Scala was

due to stage *Aida* with Renata Tebaldi, Mario Del Monaco, Fedora Barbieri, and Cesare Siepi. In April, the opera was scheduled to inaugurate the 28th Milan Exhibition, but Tebaldi was unwell. A theatrical agency contacted Maria Callas, who had triumphed in the role both in Italy and abroad, asking her to stand in for Tebaldi. Maria accepted immediately. She thought she would at last be able to attract the attention of Ghiringhelli and the other directors, and make a name for herself in the Milanese newspapers which had until then ignored her successes.

Maria sang at La Scala on April 12, 15, and 18, but her participation at the opera house went entirely unnoticed. The newspaper *Corriere della Sera* mentioned her with a few lines and a column headline, but without comment. Ghiringhelli didn't even greet her, as he normally did with all new

"If you want to live in harmony with yourself, you have to work. Work very hard. I don't agree with Descartes: "I think therefore I am." My motto is "I work therefore I am."

artists arriving at the theater. He went to the baritone's dressing room, which was next to Maria's, but didn't stop to visit her. His behavior bespoke open hostility, and deliberate and disparaging indifference.

Maria was very upset. She was tremendously offended, but in her soul her desire to "conquer" La Scala became even stronger. She thought and thought of the various ways she could achieve this aim. Somebody told her that the only person who nobody could refuse was Arturo Toscanini. She had to find a way to contact him.

Toscanini, a living legend, was eighty-three years old in 1950. He lived mainly in the United States but exerted a powerful influence over the Milan theater through his daughter, Wally. His every wish was law and every artist he presented was welcomed with open arms. There was an obstacle, however: The great conductor was surly, reserved, and unapproachable.

This is where destiny lent Callas a hand. One day, in Parma with her husband, she was presented to Luigi Stefanotti, an Emilian businessman with a passion for opera, who said he

was a great admirer. He knew everything about her career and Maria was greatly flattered. He was a storylike figure: a determined professional who had put together an enormous fortune and was so enamored of music that he could hold his own with the most skillful artist. He knew all the great names in opera and also knew Toscanini. What was more, since Toscanini had great intuition for true lovers of music, Stefanotti was one of the few people the famous conductor listened to and admired. When the Maestro was in Italy they met frequently.

Listening to Stefanotti talk, Maria could hardly believe her ears. He was the man who could solve all her problems. She spoke to him frankly, confided to him, and explained that it was her great dream to sing at La Scala—a dream that seemed forbidden to her. "Perhaps I could overcome these adversities with the help of Toscanini," she said timidly. And Stefanotti gallantly replied: "I'll talk to the Maestro and I am sure he will help."

That meeting rekindled her hopes. Afterwards, and on several occasions, Maria said determinedly: "They don't want me, but I shall soon sing there." In the meantime, her schedule was as intense as ever. After Rome, she went to sing in Turin, Catania, and Naples, and in May left for a two-month tour of Mexico. The flight involved a stopover in New York, so Maria decided to go and see her parents.

Callas's behavior with her family was always unclear. American and, especially, Greek newspapers accused her on several occasions of having left her parents in poverty once she had become successful. Her mother, Evangelia, wrote a defamatory book about Maria, accusing her of being an unnatural daughter—cruel, insensitive, and malicious. These accusations were repeated in the world press and are still repeated in almost all biographies. But they are untrue and create a very unfair image of Maria Callas. Maria suffered terribly over these misrepresenta-

tions, even to the point where she ceased defending herself in public.

Clearly, the relationship between Callas and her mother was far from idyllic. Maria was never able to forget that she had been "Cinderella" at home and was unable to feel deeply attached to her mother and sister. At times, she pronounced very severe judgments: "I will never be able to forgive them for having stolen my childhood. In all those years when I should only have worried about growing up and playing, I was forced to sing or earn money. I have almost always treated them well: They have almost always treated me badly. I shall never forget how they exploited me. They expected me, the youngest, to support them. My mother always preferred my sister. She even tried to ruin my career by making me sing in clubs so that I would earn money more quickly." One day she wrote to her mother who had asked for financial help: "It is outrageous that you tell me about your troubles. To earn a living, I've had to go to work and you are young enough to do the same. If you do not have enough money to live, you can drown or throw yourself out of the window." Harsh words, but words dictated by anger rather than hatred. When her mother and sister were in trouble, Maria always put aside her feelings and helped the family out.

In May 1950, on her way to Mexico, Maria passed through New York. Her mother was ill and in the hospital. Her father also had heart problems. Evangelia had decided to ask for a divorce and go and live with her daughter in Verona. It was a sad situation, and Callas suffered because of it.

She was especially disturbed by the prospect of divorce. She did not want her mother to get divorced and had absolutely no intention of returning to Italy with her. From the moment she was born, she had never known peace in family life. Now that she was successful and married to Meneghini, she knew such peace, and had no intention in the world of losing it. But at the same time, she did not want to leave her mother on her own in this difficult moment.

"She was very depressed when she left New York for Mexico. She began to prepare the operas she was to perform but couldn't concentrate. Her thoughts turned constantly to her parents' misery."

The letters Maria wrote to Meneghini in this period reflect these worries. She confided her anxieties to her husband, but only a little at a time, as if she were worried they would trouble him.

She wrote to Meneghini from Mexico City on May 4: "I am rather betes as usual and now heart problems. I told my mother: 'But how can you abandon him now that he is old and ill?' Battista, she wants to come and live with me. God forgive me, Battista, but for the moment I want to be alone with you in my home. I have no intention of compromising my happiness,

Below:

1954. Maria Callas is congratulated by conductor

Herbert von Karajan.

1957. With German soprano Elisabeth Schwarzkopf.

77

worried about my mother. I wanted to bring her here with me because I need peace and help, but I am alone and full of worry. What's more, my father is also unwell. He has heart problems and hasn't been able to work for a month. He is better now, but has lost a month's salary. And now my mother is in the hospital. Why do illnesses strike poor people who can't afford to be looked after? I hope my mother will be able to leave the hospital and come here with me in ten days or so. But will she be well? Will she be able to help me?"

A few days later on May 19 she mentioned the topic of divorce and her mother's intention to live in Verona: ". . . My mother doesn't get on with my father. He is also unwell. He has dia-

my right to be alone for awhile. We deserve it, don't we? How can I tell her that I care about her but that my love for my husband is different? I will give

My mother doesn't write. My father says she is better but how can I believe him?"

"My mother always preferred my sister. She even tried to ruin my career by making me sing in clubs so that I would earn money more quickly."

her some money so she can convalesce somewhere, in the mountains or in the country. But I don't think it is right that she should leave my father now. . . In

May 29:
". . . Today I had a huge argument over *Traviata* with Caruza-Campos, the superintendent of the Mexico City

the meantime, don't you dare prepare a passport to come here. I'll kill you if you do. I don't want you to fly. I beg you. I am terrified something might happen. . . Please look after yourself. Bye, my soul, and a kiss for our lovely home."

These worries greatly affected her work. Maria was nervous and irritable: "I'm living in a state of abnormal apathy," she wrote on May 25. "My stamina is sapped by this awful climate and the ennervating altitude. The performances are going ahead pitifully. So much so that if I were in top form I would have rebelled to the point of frightening even the animals. But I lack the strength to do this. I carry on, like an idiot in the true sense of the word. . .

Theater. He says he is preparing the costumes but I won't be moved: I do not want to sing it. I don't feel up to studying two new operas. *Il Trovatore* is more than enough. I don't want to ruin everything. The climate here is awful and I can't wait to leave. My mother still doesn't write: What can have happened? Her flight ticket has been in New York for ten days. I hope she is not unwell. . . At least as far as I am concerned, this kind of life is no good. We are wasting our best years. Enough is enough. Life has so many lovely things to offer but I am not enjoying anything. I don't wear anything special. My jewels only shine in the hotel safe. My furs are pointless because it is so hot. I don't enjoy any-

thing I have without you. I've lost another seven lbs. If I carry on like this, I'll become a skeleton."

June 1:
". . . If you were to see me now, you'd be shocked. I am furious. They want to stage *Tosca*, then *Cavalleria*, then *Trovatore*. I am also mad with Baum, the tenor. He is worse than a jealous woman. He never stops insulting me. And he is furious because at the end of *Aida* I achieved a sharp flat. The audience was delirious and Baum shook with envy. I am indignant about the way everyone works here. It is now 1:30 and I've just been informed that

1956. Maria Callas in a rare bathing suit snapshot while on holiday at Venice Lido.

Opposite page, center:

1954. Maria Callas with conductor Antonino Votto in an intermission during Spontini's Vestale *at La Scala, inaugurating the 1954-1955 season. In the same season, Callas also sang* Sonnambula *and* La Traviata, *today considered—in terms of direction— to be Luchino Visconti's masterpiece.*

Side, top:

Callas congratulated by a colleague. It was at this time that Renata Tebaldi claimed in a famous interview that she had left La Scala because there was no longer any room for her once Callas arrived.

Side:

1954. Maria Callas with Luchino Visconti during rehearsals for Vestale. *The great director, who was an opera lover, was never on great terms with Antonio Ghiringhelli, superintendent of La Scala. He began working there, on Callas's request, with* Vestale.

rehearsal for *Tosca* begins at 2:30. Just imagine it, I haven't had anything to eat. . . My mother wrote a nasty letter. She says I am an egoist, that I only think about myself, that I'm leaving her to die. I am so fed up that I'm almost ready to break off all communication with her. I am as alone as a stray dog. At least there is Simionato and we keep each other company a little. We can't rehearse because there is no rehearsal room. I can tell you, everyone should be shot."

June 5:
". . . Everyone is crazy about *Aida*. Baum almost wanted to kill me. Then, just before the second night of *Aida*, he came to apologize. It seems he was worried about getting on my bad side. I'd said that if he didn't apologize I would not sing with him again. So, the prima donna came to ask me to forget everything. Loathsome. The audience shouted "We only want Aida." After more than ten curtain calls, I had to take a bow on my own. My colleagues almost died with envy. I don't know what to say to my mother. Imagine her disappointment when she hears I shan't be going to New York."

June 6:
". . . Today, at the dress rehearsal for *Tosca*, I thought I was going to faint. What has made everything even worse is that I can't sleep. I don't sleep a wink until 6 or 7 in the morning. . . But I want to see everything through to the end. Otherwise my colleagues would be only too delighted."

June 8:
". . . I broke all records this time: I didn't sleep at all until 8:30. I think I'll go crazy here in Mexico. They say it is difficult to sleep at this altitude. I find it hard to go to sleep even at home, so just imagine here. The only positive thing about this trip is that I've lost weight. I hope I can stay like this until I return, you will find me beautiful. . . My mother phoned to say she is coming. The doctor said she could travel."

June 12:
". . . You become an idiot here in Mexico. What's more, I have a rash on my face like the one I had in Rome, only worse. And to think I have to perform *Aida* tomorrow: With this wonderful complexion, I shall have to wear black to give my face some color. . . My mother arrived and we are staying together. But I am so understandably nervous that I torture the poor thing. This is the worst moment in my life. But I shall have to be patient."

Maria returned to Italy at the end of June. She was less anxious because the problem with her mother's eyes was not really as serious as it had seemed at first. The only worry remained her parents' divorce. She tried to prevent it, but Evangelia would not take her advice and went through

". . . I am mad with Baum, the tenor. He is worse than a jealous woman. He never stops insulting me. And he is furious because at the end of Aida I achieved a sharp flat. The audience was delirious and Baum shook with envy."

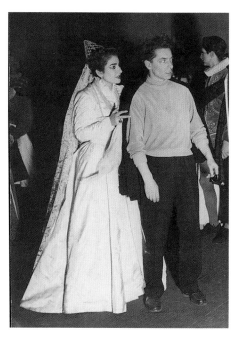

Opposite page, left:

Milan. View of the main entrance to La Scala.

Opposite page, right:

1954. Maria Callas during the dress rehearsal of

Lucia di Lammermoor *with Herbert von Karajan.*

Side:

1953. Maria Callas with Leonard Bernstein during

rehearsals for Cherubini's Medea.

Below:

1954. Maria Callas embraced by Giuseppe Di

Stefano at the end of a performance.

with the divorce. Maria indignantly said: "I don't want to hear anything else about my mother." This comment, taken up by the newspapers and repeated by her mother in many interviews, contributed not a little to confirming many people's opinion of Callas as an ungrateful daughter.

In the meantime, Stefanotti continued his diplomatic work to arrange a meeting between Callas and Toscanini. He wrote to the singer on September 10: "My Dear Lady, I need to speak with you because I have some important things to say to you. I can't write them. So that you are not unduly curious, I can say immediately that it's about Maestro Toscanini, who I talked with at length last night in his home at Pallanza."

Meneghini immediately telephoned Stefanotti, who told him that Toscanini wanted to hear Maria sing. The Maestro had a project in mind. 1951 was the fiftieth anniversary of the death of Verdi and he wanted to commemorate the occasion at Busseto with an opera staged at La Scala. He was looking for suitable singers and Stefanotti had mentioned Callas. Meneghini said that Maria would be delighted to meet the Maestro and then made an appointment. Callas received a telegram signed by Wally Toscanini on September 22. "My father will receive you in Via Durini 20, Milan, on any convenient day before his departure on the 28th. Sincerely, Wally Toscanini." Maria answered: "I shall be in Milan on Wednesday the 27th. I

shall be at your disposal for the entire afternoon."

Accompanied by her husband, Maria Callas arrived at Toscanini's home around midday. The Maestro welcomed his guests cordially but briefly, as was his habit, and while they waited for lunch the group talked in

answered: "Ghiringhelli is a complete ass and understands nothing. But Labroca is a musician and ought to understand voices."

After lunch, Toscanini began to speak of the reason why he had asked Maria Callas to come to his home. He said: "I have never in my life conduct-

the lounge. Toscanini asked precise and concrete questions. He talked with Meneghini, glancing rapidly and inquisitively at Maria. He asked about Callas's artistic experience but, in truth, showed that he already knew everything. He already knew about *The*

ed Verdi's *Macbeth* because I have never found a singer capable of interpreting Lady Macbeth. She was a character very dear to Verdi. He worked intensely on the role. He himself indicated in a letter how his Lady Macbeth should be performed: 'An ugly and

The Maestro sat down at the piano, opened the score of Macbeth, and began playing. Maria was next to him and began singing with impressive power. They went ahead for almost the entire first act. Then, stopping suddenly, Toscanini said: "You are the woman I have been looking for all these years. Your voice is what I need. I shall stage *Macbeth* with you. I shall speak to Ghiringhelli tomorrow and tell him to send you a letter of engagement."

Toscanini's enthusiasm and legitimate intention to stage her in *Macbeth* is demonstrated by the fact that he spoke immediately with Ghiringhelli,

"Everyone is crazy about Aida. Baum almost wanted to kill me.

Then, just before the second night of Aida, he came to apologize.

It seems he was worried about getting on my bad side.

I'd said that if he didn't apologize

I would not sing with him again."

Puritans in Venice, *Norma* in Florence, *Parsifal* in Rome, the tour in Argentina, and the other tour in Mexico.

At a certain moment, he asked why his guests had not already contacted La Scala. Meneghini explained Ghiringhelli's indifference when Maria sang *Aida* and the negative response of Maestro Labroca in 1947. Friends of Meneghini claim that the Maestro

malicious woman, with a bitter, suffocated, and dark voice.' I have never been able to find a singer with these vocal qualities. From what people have told me, you seem to be the person I'm looking for. I asked you to come here today to hear you sing. If what I'm told is true, we shall stage *Macbeth*. I don't want to die without having conducted this opera."

announcing that he had found the singer he needed to realize his old dream. Ghiringhelli sent a letter to Callas requesting her to be available for August-September 1951. This letter is a very important document.

Ghiringhelli's extremely polite words make it clear that Toscanini had been frank: Callas was now his protégé.

"My Dear Lady," Ghiringelli wrote to Maria Callas on October 2, 1950, "I hear with great pleasure of your meeting with Maestro Toscanini. In accord with what has already been said to you, may I kindly ask you to confirm whether you are free for the months of August and September next year. If you happen to be in Milan in the next few days, I would be most delighted to meet you. Yours sincerely, Antonio Ghiringhelli."

He was no longer hostile towards her. The superintendent had to bow to the wishes of Toscanini, and Maria was on her way to La Scala.

Stefanotti, in the meantime, continued to weave his magic. The

Macbeth project in Busseto met with enormous difficulties and was finally dropped. But, thanks to Stefanotti, Callas continued to enjoy a very cordial relationship with Toscanini. The great maestro spoke of her with considerable enthusiasm and let it be known that he was impatient to hear her sing at La Scala. And his wishes could in no way be ignored. News of the imminent arrival of Maria Callas at La Scala began to circulate, giving rise to concern throughout the international opera world. Her declared enemies by no means intended to accept defeat. And her new friends, with the exception of Stefanotti and Toscanini, were false. They put up a good face in adversity but in reality hoped for whistles and catcalls.

The prima donna at La Scala was Renata Tebaldi. A clash between the two singers was therefore inevitable. Not because they hated each other. They had met in 1947 during the famous Verona Arena Season where Maria sang *Gioconda* and Tebaldi *Faust*. But behind every famous singer there are always groups of fanatical admirers, managers, members of the press, and powerful agencies with huge financial interests. This was especially true in the 1950s, when opera was extremely popular and attracted the most important business interests in the world of entertainment.

The various clans supporting Tebaldi and Callas began their destructive work, disseminating jealousies, hatred, and gossip. And a furious war broke out between the two prima donnas, dividing Italy and filling the newspapers with dozens of poisonous articles. This war still rages today, so many years later.

In truth, this was a rivalry created deliberately by people who had nothing to do with the two artists. Renata Tebaldi was a sensitive and extremely mild woman, and quite unsuited to the role of bitter rival. And neither was Callas, despite her fierce and impetuous character, a person capable of blind and unjustified hatreds. Remarking on this topic, many years later, Callas insisted on pointing out that, in truth, at the beginning of her career, she and Renata Tebaldi were friends. "One evening in early 1948 at the Fenice Theater in Venice during a performance of *Tristan* as I was removing my stage make-up, I heard the door open and the door frame suddenly outlined the figure of Tebaldi, who was in Venice to sing *La Traviata* with Serafin. We only knew each other by sight, but on that occasion we shook hands so warmly and Renata made such spontaneous compliments that I was left enchanted. I was particularly struck by one of her comments because of certain unusual words which I, as a foreigner in Italy for only a short time, had never heard before. 'My goodness,' she said, 'if I had had to sustain such a demanding role, you would have had to scrape me up with a spoon.' I think that it is rare that two women of the same age sharing the same profession could have established such a fresh and spontaneous relationship as that which appeared between us.

"That 'feeling' became real friendship some time later, in Rovigo, where Tebaldi sang *Andrea Chenier* and I sang *Aida*. At the end of "Cieli azzurri," I heard a voice shout from a box: 'Brava, brava Maria.' It was the voice of Renata. If I may say so, we became close friends after that. We saw each other often, exchanged ideas about clothes, hairstyles, and even our repertoires."

But this affectionate friendship was sadly destroyed by people with loose tongues. As everyone spoke of her imminent arrival at La Scala, Maria continued her tireless singing marathon, performing *Tosca* in Bologna, Pisa, and even Salsomaggiore Terme. In Rome, she sang Rossini's *Il Turco*. Later, in early 1951, she performed *Traviata* in Florence, *Il Trovatore* in Naples, *Norma* in Palermo, *Aida* in Reggio Calabria and *Traviata* in Cagliari. In May, she tackled *I Vespri Siciliani* in Florence, conducted by Eric Kleiber, achieving a memorable success. On that occasion, perhaps obliged by Toscanini, even Ghiringhelli went to hear her and had to admit later that he had witnessed a very fine performance, to the extent that he immediately asked Callas to repeat the opera at La Scala to inaugurate the 1951-1952 season.

Her great moment had come. The temple of opera had thrown open its doors to Callas and she entered as a queen. The superintendent of La Scala proposed another three operas in the same season: *Norma, The Rape of the Lock,* and *Don Carlo*. What other singer on her debut at La Scala had ever been given such a program?

Maria smiled with gratification but, thinking of how she'd been shunned and ostracized, dug in her heels, and made her own demands. "Everything's fine," she said, "but I want a fourth opera: *La Traviata*." This was a touchy topic. *La Traviata* had been performed at La Scala by Tebaldi, not without some difficulty, and Ghiringhelli didn't want to give Callas the opportunity to outshine her. "No," he said, "we can't do *La Traviata*." Maria replied: "Either *La Traviata* or I won't come." Although Ghiringhelli procrastinated, he was in no position to refuse.

At the end of June, Maria Callas left for her second tour in Mexico and then went to Brazil, where she clashed violently with Tebaldi.

Maria had to sing in São Paolo and Rio de Janeiro. The cast was impressive. Serafin and Votto were the conductors and the singers included Renata Tebaldi, Giuseppe Di Stefano, Nicola Rossi Lemeni, Fedora Barbieri, Titto Gobbi, Boris Christoff, Elena Nicolai, Mirto Picchi, and Gianni Poggi—all artists of great skill and immense reputations.

Callas and Tebaldi sang the same operas, alternating. Audiences thus had the chance to admire two exceptional singers and compare their performances.

The row broke out during a charity concert that was organized spontaneously, in which all singers generously took part. During a meeting Tebaldi launched the proposal that, since it was a charity concert, all singers should sing only one piece and not

give encores. Her proposal was accepted. The concert went ahead without disruptions until Renata Tebaldi's turn came, and she sang "Ave Maria" from *Othello*. She sang this extraordinary piece better than anyone in the world, so much so that she is remembered as a superb Desdemona. The audience was enthralled; they applauded and demanded an encore. Instead of leaving the stage like all the others, Tebaldi began the encore and even performed a third. The other singers were mortified. Callas was absolutely furious. She maintained that Tebaldi had carefully prepared the trick to attract attention to herself and swore she would have her revenge.

The tour went on. Tebaldi went to sing in São Paolo, while Callas remained in Rio to continue with *Tosca*. But there was another surprise in store. The gossip was that Callas would be replaced by Tebaldi for *Tosca*'s last two performances. Someone said that Tebaldi had even ordered the costume before leaving for São Paolo. Maria did not want to believe such gossip. These performances were hers by contract. A stand-in by Tebaldi would have seriously damaged Callas's image, suggesting that she was not as important. Maria could not let this happen.

The day day before the last performance, Callas went to the opera house to read the names on the posters for the recital that evening. She saw that she had really been replaced. She went to the superintendent and argued furiously. She attacked him and threw a heavy marble inkwell at him. She returned to the hotel, packed her bags, and immediately left Brazil. Maria was convinced that Tebaldi had underhandedly arranged the substitution through her connections. It was the start of a bitter rivalry which lasted for twenty years.

Callas returned to Verona and on October 2 was visited by Ghiringhelli, accompanied by Luigi Oldani, the general secretary of La Scala. The two managers wanted to finalize the contract for opening the new season with *I Vespri Siciliani*. But Callas insisted on adding *La Traviata*. After what had happened in Brazil, she wanted, at all costs, to interpret the opera at La Scala, where Tebaldi had been widely acclaimed and adored. Ghiringhelli discussed the matter at length but Callas would not give in. In the end, the superintendent had to promise that he would do everything possible to include the opera in the program.

At the end of October, Maria sang *La Traviata* triumphantly in Bergamo. Then she went to Catania to sing *Norma* and *The Puritans*, and was in Milan for the rehearsals of *Vespri* on November 25. The opera was conducted by Victor De Sabata, a legendary figure. He and Callas immediately struck up a perfect understanding, even if, at the first rehearsals, Maria made some sharp remarks. De Sabata asked her, "Mrs. Callas, please look at me." She replied: "Maestro, why don't you look at me. Your eyesight is better than

Opposite page:

1952. Maria Callas in the leading role in Verdi's Macbeth, staged at La Scala to inaugurate the '52-'53 season. It was supposed to be conducted by Arturo Toscanini who in all his career had never tackled the work because, as he himself declared on many occasions, he had never found the right voice for Lady Macbeth. But having heard Callas, he exclaimed, "This is the voice Verdi wanted," and had Macbeth included in the program at La Scala. Health problems prevented him from conducting the opera, so he was replaced by Maestro Victor De Sabata. He and Callas immediately understood each other, even though Maria made a famous remark during rehearsals. De Sabata asked her, "Mrs. Callas, please look at me." She replied: "Maestro, why don't you look at me. Your eyesight is better than mine." Callas was notoriously short-sighted.

Side:

1953. Maria Callas in the dressing room at La Fenice Theater in Venice, in the role of Violetta, the main character in Verdi's Traviata, receiving the last touches to her costume before going onstage.

mine." Callas was notoriously short-sighted.

All of Milan's finest and most famous attended the first night of *Vespri*. Admirers and enthusiasts came from all over Europe and America. The success was astounding, applause unconditional, and the critics unanimously enthusiastic. The leading critic of the time, Franco Abbiati, who until then had always ignored the work of Callas, was forced to write in *Corriere della Sera*: "The miraculous throat of Maria Meneghini Callas did not trem-ble from prodigious extension and sounds, especially in the low and middle keys, singing with a phosphorescent beauty, agility, and technique rarely to be heard."

Regardless of this triumph, Maria did not forget her argument with Ghiringelli over *Traviata*. She continued to bombard him with telephone calls to find out when it was scheduled and Ghiringhelli continued to be evasive. Maria then threatened not to sing *Norma*. Ghiringhelli, under pressure, promised to stage *La Traviata* the fol-

"I think that it is r

of the same age sharing

have established such

relationship

developed betwee

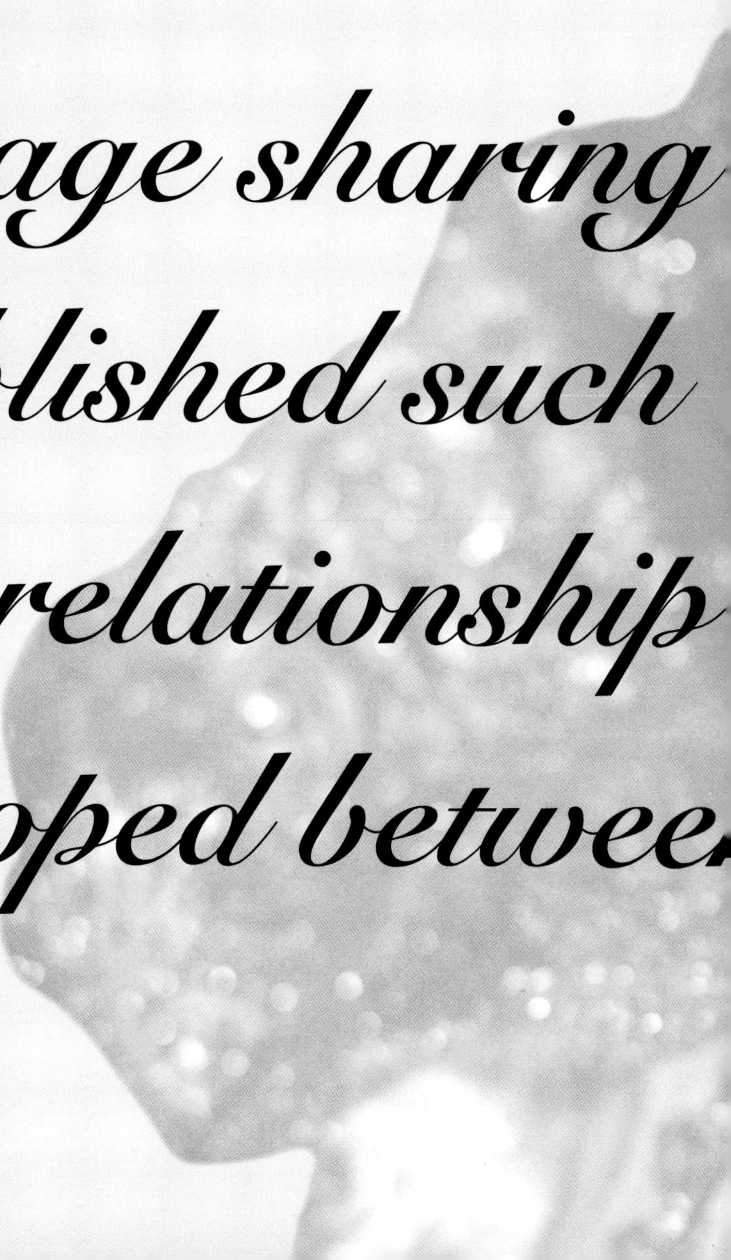

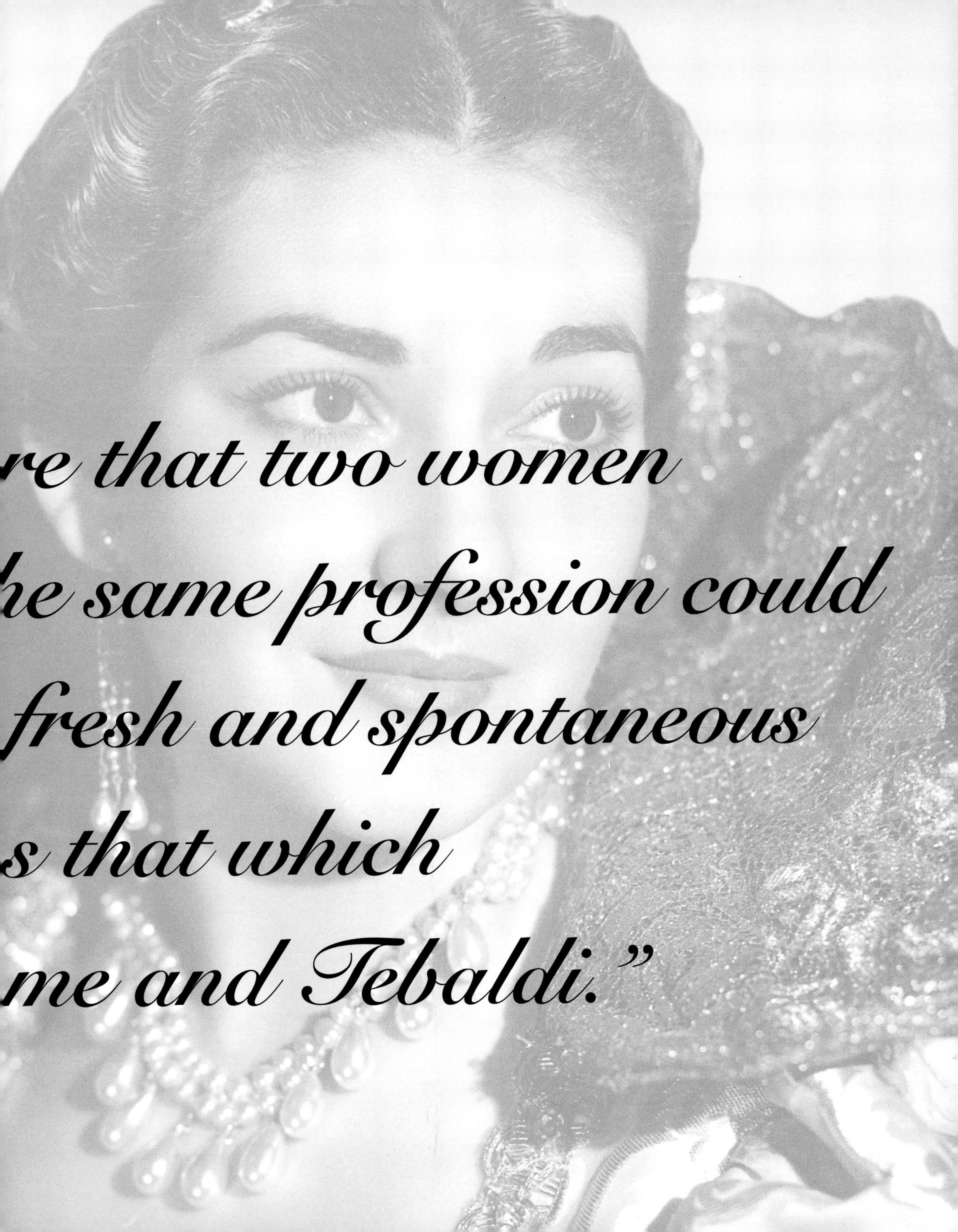

re that two women

he same profession could

fresh and spontaneous

s that which

me and Tebaldi."

lowing season. He paid out one million four hundred thousand lire without a receipt and—to justify the expense with the Board of Directors—increased the fee for the operas Callas was yet to perform.

This was how the Callas Age at La Scala began—far from serenely. But it was a golden period that lasted seven years. In this period of time, Maria sang 181 times in the Milan theater in twenty-three different roles, playing an enormous part in the increasing international prestige of La Scala. The Callas Age made history and lives in the recordings of these performances, still sold all over the world.

Once she had arrived at La Scala, Maria, guided by Meneghini, did more than sing. She was now playing a larger role in the entire production of each opera. Before accepting a role, she discussed the other interpreters, the conductor, and the director. To find out who was going to conduct the orchestra, she asked (using a phrase learned from Maestro Tullio Serafin): "Who's the baton man?"

The year 1952 was full of work. After *I Vespri Siciliani*, Callas sang *Norma* at La Scala, *The Puritans* in Florence, *Traviata* in Catania, *Armido* in Florence, *The Puritans* again in Rome with Giacomo Lauri Volpi and, lastly, made a third tour of Mexico, where she sang five operas with Giuseppe Di Stefano, discovering the extraordinariness of the tenor's voice.

achieving yet another success.

Renata Tebaldi complained, and her supporters protested. There was no longer room for her at the Milan theater. It was therefore decided that she should open the 1953-54 season with *Wally* by Catalani. Tebaldi sang very well but the opera did not draw audiences. The second opera in the program was *Mitridate*, but this staging also ran the risk of boring audiences. Someone had the idea of replacing it with Cherubini's *Medea*, an opera in

In 1953, Callas achieved yet another feat, not in the theater but at home. She transformed herself completely. She lost a dramatic amount of weight, which had all the world's newspapers talking. She was no longer matronly, but like a butterfly.

The fact that she was heavy had been a problem for Maria from the time she first sang in Greece. Many have

Callas admired the intelligence of Visconti.

She was fascinated by his art but couldn't stand his rather vulgar

language. "When you talk like that it turns my stomach,"

she often said to him.

Returning to Milan, she asked Ghiringhelli to stage *Gioconda* at La Scala with Di Stefano. The tenor had argued with the Milan theater and had been asked to leave. But Maria made sure he was engaged again.

That summer, she returned to sing again in the Arena in Verona, with two operas: *Gioconda* and *Traviata*. She made her debut in London with Norma and, as already mentioned, inaugurated the Scala season with *Macbeth* in December, conducted by De Sabata,

which Maria had triumphed at the May Music Festival in Florence. Callas in *Medea* at La Scala achieved even greater success. The comparison between Tebaldi in *Wally* and Callas in *Medea* was inevitable. Renata was skilled and gutsy but the opera was not overwhelming. Tebaldi became demoralized and soon after left Italy to settle in America. In an interview, she herself said that she had left La Scala because, with the arrival of Callas, there was no longer room for her as well.

Opposite page, top:

Milan, 1954. Maria Callas at a restaurant with Beniamino Gigli. Standing between them is Luigi Stefanotti, an industrialist from Parma, who was an opera enthusiast and helped Callas arrive at La Scala.

Opposite page, bottom:

1955. Maria Callas strolling with her husband.

Side:

Maria Callas as Cio Cio San in Madame Butterfly *by*

Puccini in Chicago.

Above:

1952. Maria Callas, with friends, leaving La Scala after a performance.

written that she was overweight because she couldn't restrain herself from eating. This is untrue. She followed strict diets but lost little weight, only to put it on again. In 1945, in America, she attempted a drastic diet. "I went from 218 lbs., to 170," she wrote. "Later, after arriving in Italy, I lost another 20 lbs. or so. This was my weight when I sang *Turandot, Tristan* in Venice, and *Norma* in Florence. After the appendix operation, at the end of 1948, I put 20 lbs. back on again. Around 1950 and 1951, I put weight on without any reason."

Her weight, besides making her heavy and clumsy, caused her circulation problems, especially in her legs. If she remained standing for several hours at a time, her ankles swelled enormously to become as large as her calves. From time to time, she suffered from abscesses which formed in different parts of her body. She had rashes like eczema, and often itched all over her body.

Meneghini was worried and had her visit various specialists, who did not know how to diagnose her. Elena Rakowska advised her to see Professor Coppo, a specialist in conditions of this sort, who said: "You are perfectly healthy. If there is anything wrong, it's in your mind. You artists are all a little crazy. You are more of an artist than the others, so you are also a little more crazy." The majority of doctors in any case were reluctant to prescribe medi-

even wrote that her mother found her with a sausage in her mouth when she was only three months old. And that, as she grew up, to ward off hunger pangs, she went into the kitchen after lunch to boil a pot of potatoes to eat in the afternoon. Sheer nonsense. As already mentioned, when she was studying in Greece, she often left home without having breakfast and her mother would run after her down the stairs to give her at least a slice of toast. In Verona and Milan, her diet was based on grilled meat and raw vegetables without condiments. No liqueurs, very little wine, never sweets. She loved rare steaks, filets and T-bone steaks. Before performing at La Scala, she would eat a filet weighing eight hun-

dred grams (1.75 lbs.).

She loved cooking but only cooked for others. She read many weeklies and always cut out the recipes and kept them in a notebook. She cooked something tasty for Meneghini every day but

Visconti stated: "I directed this Traviata for her, only for her. Not for me. I wanted to be the director to serve Callas, because it is right to serve Callas."

cines because they were unsure of the consequences they may have had on her voice.

Maria suffered from this situation. She did not like herself and dressed plainly, in dark colors, which aged her. She was reluctant to be photographed. She weighed herself every day. She even carried scales in her luggage because she was worried those in hotels would be inaccurate.

It has been written repeatedly that she had an enormous appetite, that her weight was the result of bad eating habits picked up as a child. Someone

didn't eat much herself. She asked for a large bathroom in her home in Verona and there she took electric massages and baths of every kind to try and lose weight. In a letter from Mexico written in May 1950, she told Meneghini: "I've begun a course of electric massages. It seems to help. I would like to lose a little more weight from my sides and legs."

The problem, then, was serious and important but she couldn't find the solution. Yet, in 1953, the miracle occurred. An inexplicable and unprecedented fact. Maria visibly lost weight: In just a few weeks, she shed over sixty lbs. In general, such sudden weight loss is bad for appearance: The skin of the face becomes soft and saggy. Yet Maria managed to lose weight without this drawback. Her complexion remained firm, smooth, and fresh.

There were many versions to explain this loss of weight. The newspapers used their imaginations. They interviewed specialists and each one had a personal opinion. It was written that Maria had undergone secret treatment involving stiff diets, that she had even gone to Switzerland where a famous doctor advised her to swallow tapeworms, and Maria followed his advice, downing the slimming parasite in a glass of champagne. Maria's own

She had written in 1948: "I want the best of the best. Even what I wear should be the best available." But, given her physique, she had never before been able to realize this dream. Now, finally, she could. She began to frequent the leading designers and chose the enormously famous Biki as her personal stylist. She became an extremely elegant woman and even set trends.

And the great directors, fascinated by her beauty and elegance, began to court her unabashedly—especially Luchino Visconti, the most intelligent, sophisticated and genial of Italian directors.

Visconti began to admire Callas in Rome, where she sang in *Parsifal* in

version told to close friends is far more prosaic. One evening, while she was performing at La Scala, she went urgently to the bathroom and passed an interminably long tapeworm. It seemed that she had picked up the parasite through her habit of eating raw meat. Yet the tapeworm, instead of causing her to lose weight, had the opposite effect, making her swollen and fat. Having expelled the parasite and despite continuing the same diet as before, she began visibly to lose weight. And in just a few months achieved the silhouette of a fashion model.

The great singer and artist also became a beautiful woman, and Maria finally showed her taste for elegance.

1949. Since then, whenever he could, he went to see her performances. When he couldn't go to the opera, he sent her telegrams. He began to pay her visits and they shortly became friends.

It was even said that Maria was in love with Visconti. Franco Zeffirelli, then Visconti's assistant and a friend of Callas, told us: "Maria was certainly a little infatuated with Visconti. Luchino was an exceptionally fascinating man. He could have seduced the Queen of England. He was an irresistible Casanova, a calculating Don Juan. He loved to manipulate important women and play with their sentiments. He used a very refined technique, which never failed to achieve its end. The

Opposite page, left:

1955. Maria Callas in the role of Traviata in the famous performance in May that year at La Scala, directed by Luchino Visconti and conducted by Carlo Maria Giulini.

Opposite page, right:

Milan. Maria Callas during a recording.

Side:

1954. Maria Callas, in a historic photo, discussing with three of the greatest conductors of the century: Arturo Toscanini, Victor De Sabata, and (back to the camera) Antonino Votto.

Above:

1954. Maria Callas with Franco Zeffirelli after the performance of Tosca *at Covent Garden, London.*

women who fell for him included some as famous as Coco Chanel, Elsa Morante, and others whose names I cannot mention because they are still alive. He courted Maria without respite, with flowers, letters, and presents, until she lost her head. But, as ever, once he had achieved his aims, he lost interest."

Callas admired Visconti's intelligence, and was deeply fascinated by his art, but could not tolerate his rather vulgar language. "When you talk like that it turns my stomach," she often said to him. And he replied: "People are stupid, you have to be clear." Visconti used particularly coarse epithets, especially with women. Maria shook when she heard them. "If you ever dare talk to me like that I'll give you such a slap it'll break your teeth." And Visconti knew she was serious. He never, ever spoke to her with even the slightest lack of respect.

Ghiringhelli did not like Visconti; hence, he had never been able to work at La Scala. But Maria insisted, and the first engagement he was given at La Scala was to direct the ballet *Mario e il Mago,* for which he wrote the score based on a story by Thomas Mann. But in the end it was not staged.

Visconti was obsessed with the idea of staging *La Traviata* at La Scala with Callas. He often asked to do so, saying that he would make operatic history with Callas. He was worried that another director would achieve this before him.

One day, Maria told him that she had been asked to perform *La Traviata*

Opposite page, top:

1954. Maria Callas with Beniamino Gigli during a radio concert in San Remo.

Opposite page, below:

1955. Maria Callas and Giuseppe Di Stefano, in a pub in Berlin, toasting the triumph of Lucia di Lammermoor at the Staatsoper.

Side:

Maria Callas on holiday at the seaside. The singer loved swimming and sun-bathing, convinced that

both were immensely beneficial for her skin.

Above:

1952. Maria Callas with Walter Legge, director of the recording house EMI-Voce del Padrone, and Maestro Victor De Sabata during a recording at La Scala in Milan.

for television. Visconti was extremely worried. He wrote to Meneghini on June 19, 1954, naturally to ask him to persuade her against the project:

". . . How can Maria be seduced by such a dangerous and absurd proposal? I'm not speaking out of egoism or jealousy. But have you ever seen a show on television? Especially opera? They are the ugliest, most awful and unartistic events that you could ever see. . . First of all, there are the technical limitations of television: horrible views, abysmal photography, unrelieved grayness, no soul, no vigor. . . Performances where pseudo-directors, yearning for boldness and originality, confuse theater and cinema, opera with documentary films. . . And what is worse, in an attempt to achieve a fastidious interpretative vitality (which they think is genial), they move the cameras in a way that makes you sea-sick. . . You know that they film opera with playback? The opera is already sung and recorded in advance, after which the singers (I can see Maria!) repeat the whole opera (stagewise) moving only their mouths! These are things not suited for a real artist. . . You may tell me: 'Mind your own business and we'll mind our own.' But I am stubborn and insist, with true feelings of friendship and admiration for Maria, on advising her not to tackle such a thing. It would only damage her. . . And then, precisely *La Traviata*. Go and destroy that piece which must be Maria's interpretive masterpiece, her landmark, her 'Ninth Symphony'? Send me to the devil, but I wouldn't consider myself a friend if I did not tell you my opinion."

Visconti continued writing letters to Callas, speaking to her of his project for *La Traviata*. In the summer of 1954, Meneghini informed him that Ghiringhelli had agreed to let Visconti work at La Scala with Maria. The first opera they did together was Spontini's *La Vestale* which opened the 1954-55 season. It was followed by *Sonnambula* and, in May, finally, the opera which was Visconti's dream: *La Traviata*.

Preparations were long and meticulous. The rehearsals were exhausting, Maria let herself be guided by Visconti, but never dominated. She repeatedly stated that *La Traviata* was taught to her by Serafin, saying that interpreting a work well requires a deep understanding of the score. For this reason, she followed Visconti, but was particu-

larly attentive to Maestro Carlo Maria Giulini, who conducted the opera. Visconti said: "I directed this *Traviata* for her, only for her. Not for myself. I wanted to be the director to serve Callas, because it is right to serve Callas."

Maria, Visconti, and Giulini dedicated weeks of feverish work to prepare every detail. Immediately after the first night, Giulini said: "For an instant my heart stopped beating. I was stunned by the beauty of what was before my eyes. The scene was the most refined and seductive I had ever seen in my life." Later, this *Traviata* became a legend. But in the period after the debut, the critics were ferocious. Especially against Luchino Visconti, guilty of "disfiguring and profaning" Verdi. His direction was considered "irreverent and vulgar." The critics particularly attacked him for having had Violetta take off her shoes on stage, throwing them away before "Sempre libero" at the end of the first act, and then having her die as she drops to the ground still wearing her hat and cloak.

So absorbed by the fury of denigrating Visconti's direction, the critics, at least for once, spared Maria Callas. In truth, on this occasion, even those who generally wrote poor reviews about her were benevolent and admitted that Callas had given a fine performance and that, in a certain sense, had even saved the Verdian spirit of the opera. The critic of the newspaper *Il Sole 24 Ore*, summarizing the general opinion of his colleagues, wrote: "But that pureblood of scenic art, Maria Meneghini Callas, proved able to return *La Traviata* to that climate of passion

Opposite page:

1953. Maria Callas in an evocative scene from

Cherubini's Medea *at La Scala.*

Center:

1955. Maria Callas with bass Boris Christoff in

Medea *at the Rome Opera Theater. In this role,*

Callas also had the opportunity to highlight her

exceptional acting gifts. But many critics, especially

those of the old school led by Guido Pannain,

claimed she was not suited to the role.

Above:

1952. Maria Callas with champion cyclist Gino

Bartoli at the end of a performance of The Puritans

at the Comunale Theater, Florence.

and sweet palpitation that would have otherwise been destroyed by the director."

In the newspaper *Corriere d'Informazione*, Eugenio Montale wrote: "It would require many pages to describe what Callas achieved in *"Dite alla giovane,"* and her stupendous comportment which opened *"Gran Dio morir s'giovine"* and a dozen other unforgettable pieces. Formidable. Callas has everything needed to be a great Violetta. No other artist brings together all her qualities of coloring soprano, a very rare and perhaps entirely new species."

Visconti always considered this *Traviata* his masterpiece. He spoke continually about it and often in letters to Meneghini. In August 1955, he heard that Voce del Padrone intended to record the opera with Di Stefano and a soprano other than Callas. He was indignant. He wrote to Meneghini: "A recording of *Traviata* without Maria! If it were not so huge we'd have to hold our stomachs from laughing. I am astonished that Voce del Padrone could play such a trick on Maria, undoubtedly instigated by someone else. And I cannot but think that La Scala has something to do with it. . . You never realize what imbeciles people are until it hits you over the head. . . The under-handedness seems to me to be clear, offensive, disrespectful, ungenerous, ungrateful. . . in short, everything appears to me to be so cowardly that it is not a little loathsome. . . Even this episode seems to verify the preconceived and organized hostility against Maria. And against *La Traviata* in May. Against an event which, in its perfection, disrupted the mediocre, the obtuse, the jealous, everyone who felt and foresaw the collapse of their entire wretched world of convenience, routine, and mental laziness! Threaten never to sing at La Scala again, threaten to sing elsewhere!"

This was prophetic, as we shall see. In reality, Maria was merely tolerated at La Scala. She was "the queen" of audiences, but not for theater management.

As well as Visconti, Zeffirelli, another great Italian film director, was also enthusiastic about Maria Callas. Maria held Franco in high esteem, and cared about him. She met him in 1950 when she sang in *Turco in Italia* in Rome. Zeffirelli was young and good

company, and Maria said of him: "I like that young man, all fire and nerves, he will go a long way." Franco followed all Maria's performances and sent her enthusiastic letters and telegrams. He also had the idea of producing *La Traviata* with Maria. However, his ambition was not so much to direct a theater performance as to make a great film. He had found financing and had organized the executive team. The selected orchestra was the London Philharmonic conducted by Victor De Sabata. The staging and musical consultation were to be entrusted to Susi Cecchi d'Amico and Fedele d'Amico. Visuals and color were to be the work of Lila De Nobili, while photography was to be covered by Giuseppe Rotunno. The schedule had also been planned. Every time Franco met Maria or wrote to her, he always spoke of this project.

"I think that our idea to film *La Traviata,* he wrote to her, "is something very serious and this is why I have worked for so long to put it into action. I think that I shall suffer from atrocious regret for the rest of my life if we cannot capture your *Traviata* on three thousand meters of film. The idea for this film, and I will never tire of repeating it, is based on this moral necessity: Produce a living and perfect document of one of your great interpretations at your peak as a great artist, in the years of your most splendid womanhood. I

want the film to travel the world, to the most forgotten and far-flung places, from Patagonia to the Congo, so that everyone can see it and, tomorrow, for goodness's sake, future generations will have what neither Duse nor Bernhardt were able to leave behind them. The document of this exceptional creature, who has moved, exalted, and delighted trembling audiences and peoples in this troubled half of the twentieth century."

Star of

The historic *Traviata* at La Scala at the end of May 1955, directed by Luchino Visconti and conducted by Carlo Maria Giulini, created such a stir that Callas immediately became a star. Radio, television, newspapers, and magazines began to treat her as if she were a Hollywood star.

With this opera she demonstrated that she not only had a unique voice and incomparable singing technique but also marvelous interpretative skills. She was also extremely attractive: slim, slender, and with a silhouette the envy of top models. Stylists and fashion designers were at her feet; directors and conductors argued with each other to work with her; photographers and journalists attempted to immortalize her in photos or interviews; the jet set opened its arms. She was at home with Prince Ranier of Monte Carlo and a personal friend of Grace Kelly, Ingrid Bergman, and Marlene Dietrich. In short, she had become one of the most popular and most famous women in the world.

he Opera

Yet the world of opera continued to snub her. She was fiery, intelligent, aloof, and independent; she saw things in her own, highly personal and stubborn way. And in mayhem typical of the times—where chauvinistic superintendents, conductors, and directors were accustomed to making the rules, dominating singers, imposing their own protégés, and destroying the careers of anyone who dared rebel—Callas made many enemies.

Politically, she had no patrons and supported no party. She had her own ideas and convictions. She was against the Communists because, in Greece immediately after the War, they had dismissed her from the Royal Opera House in Athens. She despised the fascists, as we have seen in her words written from Argentina (especially the phrases used about Perón and Evita). She was somewhat racist about southern Italians, who she considered lazy troublemakers. "I swear and swear again that I will never again set foot in southern Italy," she wrote while singing at the Teatro Massimo in Palermo. And when she was in Naples, she wrote to her husband: "Every day, in the afternoon, I have a lot of free time. I would like to go to the cinema but I am frightened about the hangers-on."

In 1954 Pope Pius XII, who was a music-lover and an expert on Wagner, expressed his wish to meet Callas after hearing her sing in *Parsifal* on the radio. But Maria, although she was religious, did not rush to the Vatican as many would have done in her place. The pope had to invite her a second time before she agreed to meet him. During the

audience, they spoke of music and she calmly contradicted him, much to the shock and surprise of the monsignors present.

She was a strong and free woman. Her serene and solid married life provided her with stability and certainty. The home, for Callas, was an impregnable fortress. When she returned from touring internationally, she locked herself at home and felt like a true queen. She adored and trusted her husband,

ed, she no longer wanted to see them. Meeting Ingrid Bergman, who had just split from director Roberto Rossellini, she said coldly: "We can't now be as

When young and obliged to travel alone, she wrote long and passionate letters to Meneghini, as we have already seen. Now that she and her husband always travelled together, she wrote no more. But she habitually left little love notes around the house for him to find.

From the time they had first met, Maria would give her husband three flowers or three bunches of flowers, with a meaning that only the two of them knew about.

"Three flowers. Only you know what this means. Put them in your office and let them bring you all the goodness there is in this ridiculous world."

But if idyllic peace reigned in Maria's home, tempests blew outside. Enemies and jealous colleagues, simmered and looked for every opportunity

"You will soon tire of reading notes from your Maria but I cannot but send three bunches of flowers. It has been a tradition for seven years, and I wouldn't dream of changing this habit. My darling, care for me as much as I care for you. I ask for nothing else. Your loving wife."

never once considering the possibility of betraying him. She was intransigent on this point. When she heard that friends betrayed their husbands or were separat-

friendly as before."

She was very tender with Meneghini. The tiger that roared in theaters was as sweet as a lamb at home.

to attack and destroy her. The situation became explosive, and Callas was drawn into a vortex of complaints and rebellions, much of which was brought about by her own behavior. She was arrogant, intransigent, fiercely competitive, and determined to dominate her field—everywhere and at all costs.

Maria was in demand in all theaters but it was difficult to satisfy her. Before signing a contract, Maria made sure that the opera was of her liking, with other singers she liked, and conductors she could get along with. Above all, this had to include a suitable fee. In the golden years of her career, she was the most highly paid opera singer in history. Neither Caruso, nor Tamagno, nor Gigli, nor any other opera singer earned as much as she did. She could ask for ten thousand dollars for a single concert, while her other highly renowned colleagues sang for half.

One day, in Milan, she was doing a photo shoot for *Harper's Bazaar.* The photos were to be taken in the room where Verdi had lived in the Grand Hotel et de Milan. Jeweller Faraone had loaned an antique emerald broach; since it was extremely valuable he had hired a private detective for surveillance. Maria was annoyed by his presence and asked that he leave the room. "He has to keep an eye on the jewels," she was told. "Well, I shall buy them," she replied, throwing a withering glance at the person. "Now that they are mine, everyone OUT!"

She wore only designer clothes and her wardrobe was worth a fortune.

Newspapers claimed she owned twenty-five fur coats, forty evening gowns, one hundred and fifty pairs of shoes, two hundred two-pieces, and three hundred hats. Photos of her jewels were published in magazines in articles six or seven pages long. When she entered a shop, she hired a model to try on the clothes she intended to buy so that she wouldn't tire herself too much. Newspapers stated that she spent entire afternoons with beauty consultants for treatment with creams, oils, electric massages, and perfumes.

Having become queen of La Scala, Maria wanted to conquer the rest of the world. In America, she had already sung in Chicago in 1954, but her goal was the Metropolitan in New York. There were two reasons for this: It was the most prestigious theater in the world after La Scala, and Renata Tebaldi was achieving astonishing success there. Winds of war blew between the two singers, as we have seen. And the newspapers willingly stirred up the flames of their argument. *Time* published this comment by Maria Callas: "Renata Tebaldi is a spineless artist." And Tebaldi immediately rejoined: "It may be that I do not have a spine but I have something that Mrs. Callas doesn't have: a heart."

The Metropolitan was governed by Rudolf Bing, a famous English impresario of Austrian origin who had worked in Vienna, Darmstadt, Berlin, and Glyndebourne. An authoritarian, he was convinced that singers should be honored and grateful to have even been considered by him. As soon as he had been appointed superintendent in New York, he had tried unsuccessfully to engage Callas and subsequently decided

nerve-wracking negotiations, but Bing had no alternative but to accept Maria's conditions. She was to open the 1956-57 season with *Norma*, followed by *Tosca* and *Lucia di Lammermoor*, all operas in which she excelled.

The opening night for *Norma* was set on October 29, 1956. Maria was joined by Fedora Barbieri, Mario Del Monaco, and Cesar Siepi, under conductor Fausto Cleva. The opera was hugely successful, even if Maria was by now the center of much controversy. A few days before the debut, Maria appeared on the cover of *Time*, but the article inside was poisonous, unveiling many of her defects and revealing scandalous private information about her. The magazine had sent reporters to Greece, Italy and Buenos Aires to interview people who had known Maria before she became famous. Her mother and sister were also involved. The magazine claimed that she left them to live in poverty. Her father refused to take part in this absurdity but her mother accepted, telling journalists, crying, that she at least wanted to see her daughter on stage but didn't have the money to buy a ticket. The American press gave Maria a dreadful reputation and gleefully awaited her fall.

Maria did not anticipate such an attack and the article ruined her debut in New York. She was indignant, bitter, and wanted to pack her bags and return to Italy without singing. It wasn't easy for Meneghini to calm her down and convince her that fleeing would only have made things worse.

In the meantime, the article in *Time* was taken up by the press in half the world, as well as by Italian newspapers.

four points. She wrote in English and then translated it into Italian, to send to *Time* and *Corriere della Sera*. Reading it, one notes a calm, reserved style—free of anger and rancour. But Maria's troubled soul was all too evident.

Maria was especially upset because *Time* had ridiculed her husband, presenting him as somewhat of a caricature. "It is not true that my husband, as a sign of love, sprinkled flowers around my bed every evening. It is a ridiculous story. Nor is it true that he asked me to stop singing. If he had ever asked me this, I would not have sung again."

She dealt with some episodes concerning La Scala at length. *Time* had written that on one occasion she had

said: "La Scala is a magnificent theater but I am short-sighted, and for me all theaters are the same." She retorted: "The story about La Scala and my short-sightedness is ridiculous. It was invented by the usual polemic journalists who did not like the idea of my being at La Scala. Things I have said in another manner are quoted and distorted."

Regarding her rivalry with Tebaldi, she stated: "Tebaldi has never been my victim. Perhaps the opposite is true. It is not true that I live by comparisons. I hate them. But defending oneself and coming out victorious is not a fault but something good. But that doesn't mean I enjoy battles."

Time also insinuated that, having argued with conductor Serafin, Callas had made sure that the old maestro lost contracts with a record house for a number of recordings. "It is not true that

"It is not true that my husband, as a sign of love, sprinkled flowers around my bed every evening. It is a ridiculous story. Nor is it true that he asked me to stop singing. If he had ever asked me this, I would not have sung again."

not to bother with her again. But Maria's fame was growing greater and greater. Toscanini spoke of her everywhere and everyone wondered why Bing was unable to bring her to the Metropolitan. Bing was forced to track her down to avoid damaging his own reputation.

An agreement was reached after

Corriere della Sera, in particular, gave the story significant coverage. Following the newspapers' lead, the weeklies and magazines also began to deal with the topic. Maria never ceased repeating that the article was full of lies and decided to publicly deny it. She wrote in her own hand a denial comprising twenty-

Serafin was pushed aside from these recordings by me," wrote Maria. "It is absurd to accuse me of such things."

Time quoted her as having said: "I understand hatred and respect revenge." She replied: "I have never uttered those words. It is ridiculous and quite unlike my way of thinking. I could say that I hate revenge and whoever puts it into practice doesn't understand hatred."

As regards her desire always to take curtain calls alone after performances, she wrote "It is not true that I want all the applause after a performance. On many occasions I have insisted that colleagues accompany me, and they often had no right to do so. Such as Di Stefano, in Lucia, on the first night at La Scala;

Infantino in Lucia in Venice; Del Monaco in the last performance of Andrea Chenier at La Scala. You can ask all three of them and see if they dare contradict me."

She denied that her husband had spent a fortune to launch her career. "He spent money on my clothes and jewels," she wrote. "But no one becomes famous because of her husband's money." And she concluded: "It is not true that I said what is reported at the end of the article, i.e., 'People would like to see me slip up at least once. Well, I cannot and will not slip, I will never give this satisfaction to my enemies.' These are words of mine distorted beyond recognition to make me seem presumptuous and sure of myself. On

Opposite page:

Maria Callas waving as she leaves the plane in Athens in early August. It was the first time she returned home to Greece since her departure in 1945, under suspicion of having collaborated with wartime enemies (she had sung for Italian and German troops). In 1945, she had vowed never to return to Greece, but, having become famous all over the world, she accepted engagements to sing concerts in Athens and make peace with her homeland. However, she found a hostile climate amongst her countrymen, and the tour finished on a polemic note.

Side:

Maria Callas descending from an aircraft in New York on the occasion of her debut at the Metropolitan, the last great theater she had yet to conquer. At that time, the Metropolitan had already witnessed the triumphs of Renata Tebaldi.

Above:

1957. Maria Callas with her husband Meneghini in Athens during her first tour in her homeland.

103

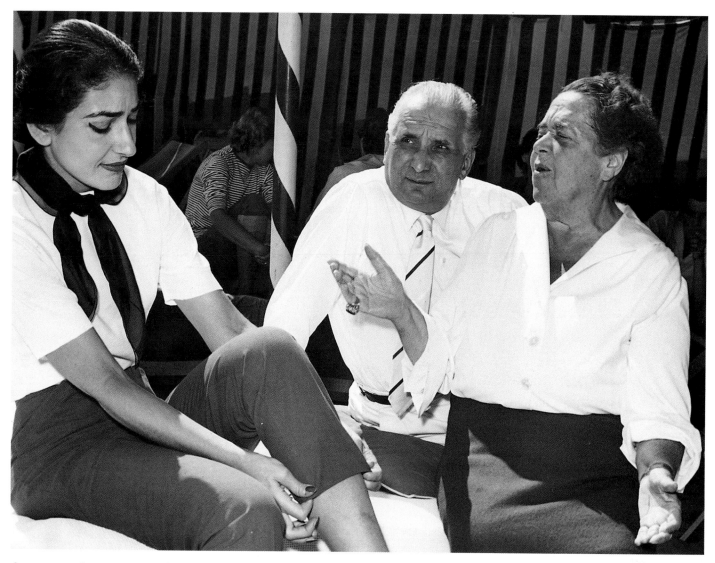

the contrary, I am a pessimist by nature."

The coalition of Callas's enemies in America was headed by Elsa Maxwell, a newspaper and TV journalist who was known as "the gossip of Hollywood." She had an immense influence on public opinion. As well as publishing her articles in a syndicate of newspapers, she had talk shows on radio and television. She was seventy-three at the time and had for some years sided with Renata Tebaldi, never missing an opportunity to attack Callas. She had written hostile articles even when Maria had sung in Chicago. After the debut with *Norma* at the New York Metropolitan, Maxwell wrote: "The great Callas left me stone cold." Her attacks continued even when Maria sang *Tosca* and *Lucia di Lammermoor* at the Metropolitan.

Maria was determined to win over this woman. It was said that Maxwell had certain "preferences," and Callas decided to play hard herself, and cater

to her wishes.

Early in December 1956, there was a huge reception in New York offered by a Greek shipping magnate, who also invited Maria Callas. Maria went along happily because she knew that Elsa Maxwell would also be at the party and found a way to be introduced to the journalist during the evening. By the end of the party, they had become friends. Nobody knows what they said and nobody knows what Maria encouraged Maxwell to think or expect. The fact remains that in her article the day after, Maxwell spoke of Callas in completely different terms than those she had used until then. "When I gazed into her extraordinary, bright, splendid, and hypnotic eyes," she wrote, "I understood that she is an exceptional person."

Maxwell had fallen in love with Callas. Maria certainly did not have the same feelings but with diabolical shrewdness had encouraged the imagi-

nation of the gossip columnist to wander at will. And so, Maxwell became a determined supporter of Maria, writing favorable articles which were published not only in America but also in Italy.

the crew and the other passengers. The news reached journalists, and the end of the friendship between Callas and Maxwell caused a great stir. American and European journalists were titillated,

"Tebaldi has never been my victim. Perhaps the opposite is true.

It is not true that I live by comparisons. I hate them.

Defending oneself and coming out victorious is not a fault but something good. But that doesn't mean I enjoy battles."

Together with these articles, she also wrote long love letters to Callas, two or three every week, some as long as ten pages. Meneghini kept them in a sealed envelope he showed to friends saying: "This is really dynamite." Unfortunately, after the death of Maria Callas's husband in January 1981, these letters were burned. "They were full of scandalous things," said the lawyer representing Meneghini's heirs. "Better to destroy them: They could ruin a lot of people."

The ambiguous story between Maria Callas and Elsa Maxwell lasted for less than a year. In November 1957, Maria gave a concert in Dallas and Maxwell met her there. Maria, however, could no longer put up with the attentions of the older woman and, sure that she was in control of the situation, decided to clarify matters. On the flight back to New York, the two of them had a furious argument which shocked both

not the least because Maxwell at the time was publishing very partisan articles about Callas and pointedly hostile pieces about Tebaldi. Maxwell was worried, as being refused by Callas was an affront she could not bear. On arrival in New York, she sent a telegram to Meneghini. "Tell Maria that if *Time* asks her, as they have asked me, whether our friendship is over, she should deny everything forcefully as I have done. I have tried to work out where this gossip originated and have discovered that it is based on the indiscretion of the crew on our return flight from Dallas. This news must be stopped."

In the middle of December, Maxwell wrote Maria a long letter, a rather sad and pathetic letter of farewell. Not of the end of their friendship, but the end of that relationship which Maxwell herself had realized existed only in her imagination. It is one of the few letters to have escaped burning after

"Maria, now that Christmas is close at hand," Maxwell wrote, "our first thought should be for peace and good-will on Earth. I have to write to you to thank you for having been the innocent victim of the greatest love a human being can feel for another person. Perhaps one day we will both under-stand this love and recall it with regret or joy. Who knows, perhaps it no longer exists. I killed it or, rather, you helped me kill it, as newborn and marvelous as it was.

"It gave you no happiness. And

my seat, the hostess said, "You shall see that Miss Callas will sit next to you." But you, Miss Callas, my friend, didn't speak to me for several hours. Yet I feel that I almost touched your heart, once or twice. But I am healed now. I leave behind a moment of madness and per-versity which fills me with disgust. I am not accusing you of anything, except for the fact that you could have prevented this feeling before it was too late. But this is all forgotten now. It belongs to the past. If we should ever meet again, we should show ourselves to be friends

Meneghini's death and is now in our archives. It is an important document because it confirms the dangerous game Maria had played to gain Maxwell's sup-

after the first few marvelous instants, it also caused me great unhappiness. Your role in life, in my opinion, is onstage. It doesn't bother me that I shall never see

"On many occasions I have insisted that colleagues accompany me, and they often had no right to do so. Such as Di Stefano, in Lucia, on the first night at La Scala; Infantino in Lucia in Venice; Del Monaco in the last performance of Andrea Chenier at La Scala. You can ask all three of them and see if they dare contradict me."

port and that Callas herself was experi-encing a period of difficulty in her career: Audiences were rebelling against the idol they had exalted and adored for years.

you again, except onstage, where you, in your genius, know how to interpret roles never before attempted by mere mortals. You killed our love that day on the flight from Dallas. Showing me to

and be kind to each other. Otherwise, people will ask what happened between us. I have kept the promise I made to you. I have been your most eloquent defending attorney and always will be. I fought your enemies. You have many enemies, Maria!

"When I arrived in Dallas, Miss Miller telephoned to tell me what I already suspected—that only half of the tickets for your concert had been sold. Miller, almost in despair, asked me what I could do. So, for the whole day, I spoke about Callas on the radio, on television and in interviews. I did this effortlessly because I loved you. It is never difficult to speak about someone you love. It is only difficult not to speak about them. But since that evening nothing happened, I suggested that I would

buy the tickets for two thousand dollars to distribute to students and teachers at the conservatory, people who are genuinely enthusiastic about music but discouraged by the price of the tickets. I am not attempting to blow my own trumpet. I am a free person and if I want to buy tickets for any artist, then I do so of my own free will. Yet, obviously, these things come out, although I had asked for the greatest discretion. . . Wherever I go, I say and repeat that we only knew each other for a couple of weeks and that you are not the kind of woman to have friendships or affections of any kind other than with your husband. This seems to me to be very clear now and makes everything much easier for both of us. . ."

Maxwell returned to the topic in

another letter. "I am no longer jealous, I no longer feel bitter, nor do I want to see you. The world will say, as in truth it is already saying, that you only wanted to use me. I deny this categorically. The little I did, I did with my eyes open, and with my heart and soul. You are great and will become even greater."

In the meantime, Maria was involved in a thorny trial in America. She was accused of contract infringement, a serious accusation. However, she was utterly blameless. She was only the victim of blackmail by a person she once believed to be a friend. Such episodes are common in the life of artists.

As already mentioned, as soon as she returned to the States in 1945, the young Callas, as she desperately sought work, met a lawyer, Edward Richard Bagarozy, who was an opera enthusiast and improvised himself as her manager and impresario. He was not a highly regarded professional—probably only interested in opera because he had married a singer, Louise, who never managed to make a career for herself. However, they were friendly people and Maria Callas enjoyed their company and became their friend.

In 1947, when Zenatello offered Maria the contract with Verona Arena, Bagarozy showed up and convinced the soprano to stipulate a representation contract with him. It was a very stiff agreement which Maria probably signed without even reading it. Through it, lawyer Bagarozy, without ever having done anything for her, became Callas's impresario.

On her arrival in Italy, she met Meneghini who immediately began to

look after her interests. In the beginning, she continued writing letters to Bagarozy which were somewhat compromising, showing that there had once been some tenderness between them, a not entirely innocent relationship. But Maria then fell in love with Meneghini and forgot all about Bagarozy. The lawyer himself ceased to show his face. In truth, he had never found Maria even the smallest part. As a manager or impresario, therefore, he had proved incompetent. But there always existed the contract Maria had signed but which she had completely forgotten.

In 1954, Maria, by now queen of La Scala, went to sing in Chicago and achieved a huge success. The newspapers presented her as the greatest living singer. She was "divine," a star in every sense of the word. It was then that Bagarozy remembered the contract. He read and reread it. He focused particularly on the clause in which it was agreed that Maria Callas undertook to pay him ten percent of all her income. He made a few rapid calculations and realized he was looking at a fortune.

real fortune in those days.

Callas was bitter and indignant. She claimed that Bagarozy had tricked her, taken advantage of her, and disappeared without taking any further interest in her life or career. And now, all these years later, he expected to be paid.

The court to which Bagarozy turned confirmed that the contract was valid and that a trial should be held immediately. But Maria had other commitments with La Scala and had to return to Italy. While waiting for a new hearing, she wrote a long memo which she sent to the court. The handwritten document was fourteen pages long. Although it may have been prepared with her lawyers, the style is the same as that of her personal letters.

The document is entitled "My Defense." Some excepts follow below.

"How can I defend myself when I am so far away from Chicago? All my interests are here in Italy and naturally I cannot come to Chicago. How can I be tried in Chicago when I am not a Chicago resident nor even a U.S. resident?

"It is not true that I said 'People would like to see me slip up at least once. Well, I cannot and will not slip, I will never give this satisfaction to my enemies.' These are words of mine distorted beyond recognition to make me seem presumptuous and sure of myself. I am a pessimist by nature."

While it was true he had done absolutely nothing to deserve the money, the law was on his side.

He would probably have accepted a large sum without demanding everything due to him. But as soon as he contacted Callas and Meneghini explaining that he wanted to be paid, he found himself faced by lawyers since Callas immediately turned the question over to her legal advisors. He then became malicious. If it was going to be a fight, then it would be a fight to the bitter end.

The episode immediately took a bad turn since the newspapers had already trained their sights on Callas and relentlessly pursued scandal. Moreover, the sum Callas was expected to pay up was enormous and big news: Three hundred thousand dollars was a

"I resided in the United States only for eight years before the war. Between January 1937 and September 1945, I lived in Greece, Athens, and since June 1947 until now in Italy, being married to an Italian.

"I cannot come to Chicago because my work does not permit me one week's rest let alone a long trip to Chicago. Until October I have not one free day and have scheduled performances every other day—plus rehearsals. The whole season at La Scala is based on my performances and will not ever permit me to leave for even two days. I have legitimate contracts and must fulfill them otherwise I must suffer all the consequences that derive from an unfulfilled schedule. So I don't see how I can be present to defend myself."

Having made these points, Maria took up the heart of the matter. Firstly, she attempted to dismantle the reliability of lawyer Bagarozy by insinuating that he was a cheat. "The court has taken this man's word for this contract, but no one has dreamed of questioning its validity. I know it is not valid because this man, since the time I was forced to sign the contract, had promised to do everything for my career . . . but has not done one single thing. The only thing he did in eight years is sue me for the intended sum.

"First, this man must prove with facts and everything that comes with it that he helped me. Second, he must prove that he is highly appreciated and esteemed (as he claims to be) in the music world. See the 1946 disaster of the Chicago season—with German, French, and Italian artists (including myself) left stranded in New York and Chicago, having to sing concerts to raise the money to return to their own countries. He is not only widely known as having been responsible for this (he was the backer and financier), but, furthermore, has a less-than-clean record. He has been accused of fraud three times. If this man is so esteemed as an impresario in Chicago, why isn't he known as such? What business does he do? Is he an active lawyer? Why did he abandon me for all these years? Why now, that I am what I am, does he ask for money and libel me in the newspapers, as he did during my stay in Chicago where I

was not visiting for pleasure but for a heavy and complete opera season? He does it only to frighten me. To force me to compensate him or, rather, pay him off as he has already done with poor Rossi Lemeni, who had to give him 7,700 dollars. I can attest that he did nothing for Rossi Lemeni. He kept him in the United States, promising him work but then gave him nothing, and caused him to waste six months in New York.

"I accuse him of defamation in saying that his wife gave me useful lessons for my career. First of all, I was already an artist, having sung for seven years at the Royal Opera Theater in Athens as leading soprano. I had an audition at the Metropolitan and refused the contract, as Mr. Johnson can testify. His wife fol-

lowed me and Rossi Lemeni to Italy in the hope of making a career but, naturally, failed completely, even though I did everything to help her. She stayed in Italy for more than a year and it was her father who helped her return to the United States because her husband didn't have the money to do so. I swear this

and I hope my word of honor is worth something.

"I would like to know why this man came to Italy a year later and did not try to find me. I heard about his trip from tenor Galliano Masini. He can attest to this fact. Everyone can but, naturally, not in Chicago. I accuse him of complete abandonment, leaving me without a penny in my pocket and one thousand dollars in debts (I borrowed from my godfather so I could travel from New York to Verona). This man took the check my godfather gave me in order to cash it at the bank and buy the tickets for the ship, saying that he knew people who could offer a discount. I never saw that money again. I don't know how much the ticket cost but surely not very much because he bought tickets for me, his wife and another poor lady. All three of us in the same cabin on a Russian ship called *Rossija*. It was horrible. I practically starved to death. We only had potatoes, butter, and a few other awful things to eat. He promised to send my money to me immediately but I never saw it again. I was forced to live in Italy with just fifty dollars in my pocket. God in his goodness helped me meet my husband, but then he was only a friend, and I didn't feel that I could ask him for money. Especially because he was the man I loved.

"I know I was silly to trust and believe in Bagarozy, but I was young and I suppose I felt sorry for him after the ruinous season in Chicago. Their financial disasters were so frequent and caused them a great deal of trouble. His wife always promised me that they would repay me. I don't like to say such things, but I have never calculated exactly how much that man had to give me back. For me, now, that money is nothing. But at the time I was in great need of it.

"I would like the court to know that

if I thought I had to give this man one dollar, I would give it to him. But he owes money to me. It is strange, isn't it, that he asks what he is asking for? I accuse him of having sold to third parties the so-called contract signed between us. How this can be allowed I do not know and I ask the court for justice."

Maria's "defense" was read and checked by the judges, who found it documented and true. The case was moving in favor of the singer. But, in August 1956, when Maria was preparing for her debut at the Metropolitan, there was a sudden, unforeseeable change of events. Bagarozy's lawyers said that their client possessed some red-hot documents. In her defense, Maria claimed that Bagarozy had ceased to be interested in her after she left New York in

1947. The lawyers claimed that this was untrue. Bagarozy was prepared to show the court the letters Maria had written to him from Italy, telling him about her situation and asking advice for her career and private life. The lawyers gave Callas's legal representatives copies of those letters. It was a low blow. These letters were widely quoted in Chapter Two and, as we have seen, were highly compromising. Meneghini did not know that his wife had continued writing to Bagarozy after her arrival in Italy. Maria had always kept the fact hidden, for a very serious reason. These letters clearly show that there had been tenderness, sweetness between her and the lawyer. If they were to end up in the newspapers, a scandal of enormous proportions would have exploded. So, Bagarozy had won. Callas's lawyers received instructions to buy the letters. A huge sum was paid, and the case was closed.

In the meantime, Maria continued singing with enormous success. In mid-January 1957, she held a wonderful concert in Chicago. Then she went to London for *Norma* and to record Rossini's *Barber of Seville*. She returned to Italy for six performances of *Sonnambula* at La Scala, and then gave six performances of Donizetti's *Anne Boleyn*, again at La Scala, conducted by Gianandrea Gavazzeni and directed by Visconti, followed by four performances of Gluck's *Iphygenia* in Tauride, again with Visconti. In June, she sang in Zurich and Rome; in July, in Cologne; and then back to La Scala to record *Turandot* and *Manon Lescaut* for "His Master's Voice."

Maria's performance was much anticipated in Greece, her homeland. Organizers had been trying for years to persuade her to give a concert in Athens, but negotiations were never concluded because of all her other commitments. Early in 1957, the Greeks asked their famous countrywoman to take part in the Athens Festival scheduled for August. Maria had one week free early in the same month and hoped to go on a short seaside holiday. She sacrificed it for love of her country.

But a cold reception awaited her. Her mother and sister had, on several occasions, given interviews in which they complained that Maria, by now very famous and very rich, never gave them even a penny. These interviews strongly influenced the general public, which became rather hostile towards her. When the news came out that she was to take part in the festival with two concerts, the tickets sold like wildfire: Many people wanted to be there to whistle and catcall.

Knowing the situation, Callas tried to be shrewd. When it came to signing the contract, she expressed her wish to not receive a fee. But the organizers felt offended by her gesture. They said that their festival had no need of subsidies or handouts. Maria was upset. In reaction, she then demanded the kind of fee she could command in America. The organizers were taken aback but didn't have the courage to protest.

This detail only increased tension and hostility. Upon leaving for Greece, Maria was physically exhausted. She was seen by doctors who told her she was worn out and needed absolute rest. But how could she refuse to go to Athens? In Greece's capital, later, she encountered one problem after another. It was tremendously hot with dry air and constant wind; her suite in the hotel was on the top floor where the wind was even more severe. Moreover, there was a building site near the hotel which caused a lot of noise and dust. Maria's health deteriorated. She was visted by Dr. Kotzaridas, who said that her throat was fine but that one of her vocal cords was somewhat sore. At the dress rehearsal, Maria realized that her voice

was not up to par and decided to skip the first concert. She informed the management so that they could find a replacement. But the organizers replied: "Either you sing, or no one sings." And the concert was cancelled.

The newspapers attacked Callas, igniting a public outrage that seemed almost like a political revolt. Callas had to lock herself in her hotel room. She wanted to return immediately to Milan but it was impossible. On August 5, in the Herodus Atticus Amphitheater, she appeared before an ice-cold audience. But she gave a magnificent performance, singing so well that the audience was enraptured.

Before leaving Greece, she sent a long letter to the newspapers in which she attempted to clarify matters and set the record straight. She explained that she was in poor health but had nevertheless wanted to honor her engagement for love of her country; that she had offered to sing free of charge; that the wind and heat had worsened her health. She also rebuked the accusations made against her by her family. Her words convinced the management of the festival, and even political dignitaries approached her in her hotel to present official apologies.

Upon returning to Italy, she was seen again by Dr. Semeraro who told her: "Without question, you must rest." "I can't, I have to leave with La Scala for the Edinburgh Festival," she answered. The doctor then wrote the following certificate: "Maria Meneghini Callas has symptoms of very serious nervous exhaustion caused by overwork and stress. I prescribe a period of complete rest for at least thirty days."

The certificate was taken to Luigi Oldani, the general secretary of La Scala, who said: "It is impossible to replace Callas. It would be better to cancel the tour rather than go without her. The assurance of her name underlies the whole contract. Maria can work miracles, as she will again this time."

So, against her doctor's advice, Maria left for Edinburgh. The contract was for August 17-30, and included four performances of *Sonnambula*. La Scala wanted five, but Maria refused the final recital so that she could go to Venice in early September to a party honoring Elsa Maxwell.

Upon arrival in Edinburgh, she discovered that La Scala had assured her presence for all five performances. So,

none of the management of the festival realized that she could not take part in

"Until October I have not one free day and have scheduled performances every other day—plus rehearsals. The whole season at La Scala is based on my performances and will not ever permit me to leave."

the final performance. La Scala had subtly manipulated her, hoping that she

would not have the courage to withdraw at the last moment. Maria kept quiet and sang superbly, so much so that the BBC elected her "queen of the festival." Yet,

having completed four nights as agreed, she packed her bags. The news of her departure came like a bolt of lightning. The art director of the festival, Robert Ponsomby, dashed to the soprano's hotel, where Maria showed him her contract. Ponsomby was astonished that the management of La Scala had not said anything to him. He indignantly went to Oldani and demanded an explanation. Oldani in turn dashed to Maria to beg her to save La Scala. "I won't save anything, you should have thought about it earlier," she replied.

The director of the festival realized that Maria was in the right. But the press and the public had to be informed. If the truth were told, the reputation of La Scala's management would be damaged. Maria was therefore asked if she didn't mind her absence being explained by health reasons. Maria was in top vocal form but agreed. A certificate was prepared that explained that Callas was leaving the festival for reasons of poor health.

However, this stratagy did not work. The press did not accept the official justification and newspapers launched a new campaign against her. She took the flight to Milan and then travelled to Venice for the party with

112

Maxwell. As soon as the news broke that Maria, instead of being ill in bed in Milan, was in Venice enjoying herself at a party, public opinion turned unanimously against her. Even Maria's own fans were angry and disapproving.

Articles attacking her were published every day. Everyone claimed she was capricious, saying that she was a star who cancelled performances unnecessarily, without any concern for the audience and the huge sums of

Edinburgh, did not believe a word she wrote, nor the medical certificates she presented. Quite the opposite. They put their case to AGMA (the Association of Opera Singers), a powerful U.S. organization created to safeguard entertainment industry interests. This organization could impose fines, suspend people from working, and even arrange boycotts of "guilty" artists to the point of excluding them from all American theaters. The AGMA was extremely strict.

money they paid to hear her sing. Everyone was against her. The damage to her image was immense.

From September 27 to November 10, Callas was engaged at the San Francisco Opera House. But, understandably, her physical and psychological state was poor; she was unable to manage the stress of both the trip and the performances. She sent the medical certificates to the theater management, asking—at least—for the performances to be postponed. But the directors of the theater, who had read the articles published following the events in

Maria's career was at stake. Reflecting on the drastic consequences of these facts, Callas decided that it was time to tell the whole truth. "La Scala must assume its own responsibilities and I demand an official statement."

She wanted the Milan theater to call a press conference and explain how things really went. She tried for weeks to arrange a meeting with Ghiringhelli, who she felt was the person entirely responsible for the episode, but he was as evasive as ever. In the end, she decided personally to write a long account of what had happened, intended for

AGMA and the newspapers. In this document, Callas summarized the facts, as outlined above, demonstrating that the entire episode arose not from her lack of professionalism, but from her "goodness." La Scala had tricked her in Edinburgh. And to save La Scala from spoiling its reputation, she accepted that her departure from the festival would be explained by ill health. This equivocation was the source of all the others. She was only the victim of everything that had taken place.

Once again, Callas was convincing. On January 26, 1958, she appeared before the AGMA Commission, which in the meantime had read Callas's account of matters and made its own investigations. Fortunately, everything worked out well. Despite deciding that her absence in San Francisco was not fully justified, they accepted the medical certificates and did not condemn her for infringement of the contract.

But her troubles were not over. Precisely at the beginning of the same month, Maria experienced another dreadful experience, perhaps the worst of her career. On January 2, 1958, Maria was to inaugurate the Rome Opera Season with *Norma*. It was a particularly important evening because the president of the Republic, Giovanni Gronchi, his wife, and other dignitaries were to attend.

The days before the performance were filled with anxiety because Maria was quite unwell. However, doctors found a suitable treatment so that she would be able to go on stage. But the human voice is not a perfect instrument. At the end of the first act, Maria said that she did not feel well and could not continue singing.

The situation was not desperate, since these unexpected events are common in all the world's theaters. The management of Rome Opera House had only to act immediately, announce Callas's relapse and invite the understudy to take her place. But the theater management had pinned all their hopes on Callas's name, without thinking of arranging an understudy. They therefore tried to convince her to continue singing.

Time passed and the wait became embarrassing. Gronchi became irritable and the audience whistled. The superintendent of the theater said to Maria: "You are a great actress and can go on even if your voice fails. Go onstage and act."

Maria realized there was nothing else to be done. She couldn't achieve the sharps and had difficulty even with mid-range keys. She had risked a false note during the "Casta diva" air and someone in the audience had shouted: "Go back to Milan, you've cost us a fortune." If she had gone back onstage with such a voice, anything could have happened. She was not to be moved.

After an hour's wait, President Gronchi and his wife left the theater. Immediately after, a speaker announced that the performance was to be suspended. Mayhem ensued. For hours, hundreds of people hung around the exit waiting for Callas, with the idea of

lynching her. Maria was forced to leave her dressing room well after midnight and reach her hotel by an alternative passage. For the whole night, groups of fanatics remained below her window, shouting vulgar insults.

The lynching of Maria Callas continued the day after in the newspapers. Everyone blamed her exclusively, and no one believed she was ill. It was said that she interrupted the performance because the applause was lukewarm and someone even insinuated that she had lost her voice because on the evening before the opening night, she had gone to parties with the Roman nobility.

"Two days before the inauguration of the season with *Norma*," she wrote in yet another self-defense, "I was in bed

with a cold caught in the theater, which was not heated. The conductor came to me and said: 'Maria, you must get better, you must sing.' So, I applied hot poultices, saw the theater doctor, took medicines, and called a nurse, saying I would probably need her assistance. I knew that my voice would not be in top form, but this was an important performance, in the presence of the president of the Republic. If I had postponed the event, I would certainly have been severely criticized just the same. I thought I would be able to get around things in some way.

"But I couldn't. The human voice is not a piano. You can never be sure it will do what you ask of it. That evening in Rome, I sang the first act but felt my voice was failing. I could achieve the low notes but I felt that the high notes were beyond my reach. I was even losing the middle registers. Whistles and catcalls do not phase me anymore—I'm not new to the enmity of the pit. This only makes me mad, and I try to sing better than ever to prove them wrong. I never interrupt a performance because of insults, but that night in Rome I simply could not sing.

"Many singers have had colds during performances and many have been replaced during the performances themselves. It happens all the time. Theaters should have understudies ready, otherwise the responsibility is theirs. Rome did neither one thing nor the other. At the end of the first intermission, management should have removed my name from the billboard. Instead, the president of the Republic was accompanied back to his box, in the hope that I would thus be convinced to continue. When they finally realized that I couldn't sing since my voice had gone, they said: 'Ok, don't sing. But you are an actress, at least go out and act.' This might be possible in some operas. But *Norma* without the soprano would be a betrayal.

"I went home to bed. The morning after, I was visited by the theater doctor, who diagnosed tracheitis and bronchitis with fever, saying that I might be able to sing after five or six days. The wife of the president of the Republic telephoned and said to my husband: 'Tell Maria that we know she was ill and unable to continue.' Unfortunately, she did not say this to the newspapers. The journalists asked for photos of me ill in bed. But I am an artist, not a showgirl, and I do not pose for photos in bed. I refused and the newspapers decided it would be better to insinuate that I was perfectly well but had lost control of my nerves because of the insults. Undoubtedly, this is a much more interesting explanation, but not the truth."

Four days later, feeling better, Callas made herself available to the the-

Opposite page:

Maria Callas next to Elsa Maxwell during a reception in New York. The soprano's husband, Giovan Battista Meneghini, is on the left.

Side:

1955. Maria Callas with Mario Del Monaco in Norma, *which inaugurated the 1955-56 season on December 7. It was another great triumph for Callas but, as was by now the case for her performances at La Scala, was equally enveloped by heated debate. Mario Del Monaco a few days later claimed in an interview that Callas, on the evening of the debut, had given him a violent kick in the shins so that she could go out alone for the curtain call and take all the applause.*

Above:

1957. Maria Callas cutting the ribbon to inaugurate the Rosetum Cultural Center, founded in Milan by the Capuchin Friars.

ater for the other performances but was told she was no longer needed: She had been replaced. Callas took the theater to court for breaking the contract. It was a very long case and was only brought to an end in 1971. The Supreme Court of Appeal not only acquitted Maria of any and all responsibility for what happened on the evening of January 2, 1958, but condemned the theater to pay damages. Callas was no longer singing in 1971; she was no longer in the news and no newspaper gave the sentence any particular importance. Thus, since then and still today, the whole episode is only spoken of in terms of gossip column scandal.

The outcome of the events at the Rome Opera House were extremely damaging to Callas's career. She never

again sang in an Italian theater. Political action against her was extremely intense. It is not known whether the president of the Republic himself demanded her vilification, or whether this was the action of members of his political party. The fact remains that politicians pressured both Rome Opera House and La Scala. Ghiringhelli received precise orders not to let Callas sing again. La Scala was then negotiating with Brussels Opera Theater for an opera with Callas in the summer of 1958. In February, the director of Brussels Theater sent a telegram to Ghiringhelli asking for confirmation of the event and its dates. Ghiringhelli replied: "We can no longer come. The Italian government has vetoed any possibility of Callas contin-

uing to travel with La Scala."

Ghiringhelli's attitude towards Maria changed dramatically. It seemed he was only too willing to terminate a relationship which had lasted many years.

"After the events with *Norma* in Rome," Callas wrote later, "I neither heard from nor saw Ghiringhelli again until I met him in early April at Biffi Scala, the famous restaurant adjacent to La Scala itself. He deliberately and publicly ignored me. Since then, he has neither spoken to me nor acknowledged me.

"However much I loved La Scala for its settings—the best in the world—I really could not sing under such conditions. Artists are guests in the theaters where they sing. Every performance is

something difficult and delicate in itself. And body and soul must be free to concentrate on just two things: the voice and the performance. If the theater where we are guests exacerbates the tension associated with the performance and adds continuous, repeated discourtesies and harassment, then the exercise of art becomes morally and physically impossible. Motives of dignity and self-defense obliged me to leave the La Scala. La Scala did not dismiss me. I left La Scala."

Despite all this, I did not want to leave during the season and give La Scala the chance to claim that 'Callas disappeared as usual.' There were continual provocations. I had been asked to sing *Anne Boleyn* to inaugurate the Milan Exhibition in the presence of the president of the Republic. For several weeks, there was obscure talk at La Scala about the dates and the details of the performance. In the end, I read in the newspaper that the opera for the inauguration of the exhibition was to be *Murder in the Cathedral*. I never even received the courtesy of an explanation.

"My last five performances at La Scala were in *The Pirate*. It is a wonderful opera with a stupendous and demanding role for a soprano.

"The Saturday before my last week, I had to undergo a painful operation.

the orders had been changed: it was no longer admissable to throw flowers. When I took the stage, the audience applauded. A very rare thing at La Scala, where applause is traditionally reserved for the end of the act. It was the beginning of a splendid performance. But perhaps this applause was simply too much for Ghiringhelli. At the end of the opera and the long ovations and curtain calls, while I was still on stage with my friends and the audience still crowding the theater, the metal stage fire-curtain was suddenly

Only my doctor and a few close friends knew of this. By now I had learned that Callas is never allowed to postpone a performance, nor even catch a cold. I was in great pain for six days after the operation because I am allergic to drugs and can't take painkillers. I could not sleep and could hardly eat. On Sunday, the day after the operation, I sang *The Pirate*. I sang it again on Wednesday. Saturday, May 31, was my last night, and I hoped to leave an ardent memory for both the audience and myself to celebrate our long relationship. For this special occasion, a group of young enthusiasts wanted to throw flowers at me at the end of the performance and asked permission to do so. They were told they could. But when, that evening, they arrived with the flowers,

dropped. In the entire repertory of artistic insults in the world of opera, there is nothing more brutal than this. It is an uncouth signal that says: 'The show is over, go home.' But just in case my friends and I missed the meaning, a fireman appeared onstage and shouted: 'The theater has ordered that the stage must be immediately cleared.' This was my last evening at La Scala. As soon as I left for the last time the theater which for seven years had been my second home, I was met by the group of young people waiting in the street to shower me with flowers. They had finally found a place to greet me as they wanted."

All these events made Callas bitter and further sapped her strength. She lacked the will to tackle great performances as in her younger days. But

theaters continued to demand titanic performances from her.

For the 1959-60 season, Rudolf Bing, the superintendent of the Metropolitan, asked her to interpret *Macbeth* and *Traviata*, two operas with quite different vocal demands. Ten years earlier, in Venice, Maria had achieved a similar feat in singing *Valkyrie* and *The Puritans*. But that was long ago, and she replied to Bing that she was not up to such a challenging program. Bing, who never wanted to be contradicted, insisted. He also believed that Callas was no

we will get going immediately." This atmosphere lasted a few days. At least she came out of this match victorious.

more than just a capricious star. He didn't think even for a moment that there could really be objective difficulties. After lengthy negotiations, he lost his temper, called a press conference and declared that he had broken off his relationship with Maria Callas.

The news was spread by agencies all over the world. The same evening, Maria achieved yet another extraordinary triumph in Dallas with *Medea* and the local newspapers took her side against the New York press. All Texas rose in her defense. To shouts of "Down with Bing," Texans even thought about a march on New York. Certain millionaires even said they were immediately prepared to finance a special performance for Callas in New York, staging *Medea* to "show those Yankees what real opera is all about." And they repeated: "Callas just has to say the word and

Opposite page, left:

1958. Maria Callas in a gown made specially for her by Milanese designer Biki.

Opposite page. Right:

1957. Maria Callas with her husband.

Side:

1958. Maria Callas at the end of a performance of Traviata *at San Carlo Lisbon, congratulated by admirers.*

Above:

1958. A close-up of Maria Callas wearing one of her famous necklaces.

A Bitt On

The year 1959 saw the end of the great career of Maria Callas. In the summer of that year, she fell in love with Aristotle Onassis and this brought about radical changes not only in her private life, but in her artistic outlook as well. The change revolutionized everything. Maria separated from Meneghini, reneging the enchantment of her sentimental past which until then she had always exalted in letters, notes, and every interview, destroying the values on which she claimed her life was built, abandoning herself to what she defined as the "great love" impersonated by the Greek shipping magnate, one of the richest and most powerful men in the world.

For him, Maria Callas sacrificed what had been the very reason for her life, until then: singing. With the final performances of *Medea* in Dallas, in

November 1959, Maria brought her period of major commitments to an end. She was thirty-six and decided to concentrate on "living and enjoying myself." Until then, she had given an average of sixty concerts, operas, and performances per year. After her meeting with Onassis, the next sixty performances were to take ten years. Music thus became merely a hobby for her. Sadly, the love and happiness for which she sacrificed music were to prove in the end to be empty—a bitter disappointment which ruined her life.

The first time Maria Callas met Aristotle Onassis was in September 1957, in Venice, at the famous party Elsa Maxwell organized for her. On that occasion, the Greek magnate, who was a friend of Maxwell's, was kind but not overly attentive. The second meeting

took place in Paris on December 19, 1958, for her famous charity concert at the opera for the "Legion d'honneur," the French Veterans Association.

That concert is still remembered as one of the most sumptuous and magnificent in the early postwar period. Callas

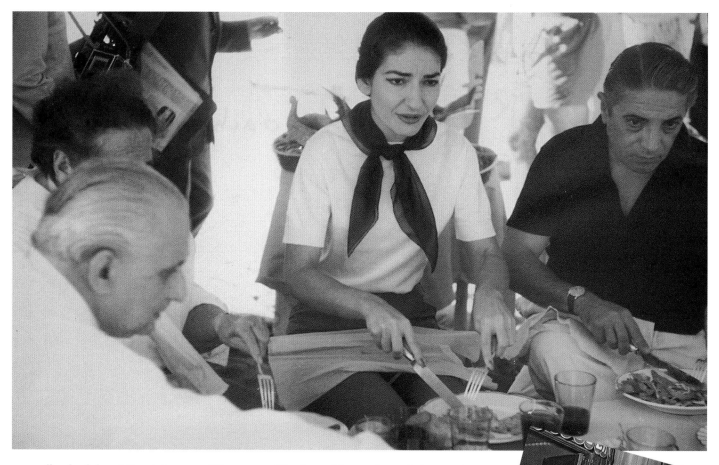

was flanked by Albert Lance, Tito Gobbi, and Jacques Mars, and the evening was conducted by Georges Sebastian. It was televised all over Europe, and praised by the press everywhere in the world.

It was a charity concert and aimed to collect as much money as possible.

The box of honor hosted the president of the French Republic, Coty; the Italian ambassador, Leonardo Vitetti; and the undersecretary for culture, Ariosto. The main theater welcomed the president of the National Assembly, Chaban Delmas; the ambassadors of Great Britain, the United States and the

"Always keep the house ready.

I may stay away a week or come back after a day.

It depends on my companions."

Maria was engaged for a fee of five million francs, a sum which had never before been paid for a single recital. The 2,130 seats at the opera were priced at 35,000 francs each and were sold in just a few days. The program for the gala event cost 2,000 francs: It weighed over two lbs. and included a biography of Callas, a record, and a ticket for the Grand Gala Charity prize draw. The event was to be followed by a dinner served in the foyer of the theater, which only 450 people could attend. Each place cost 15,000 francs.

Soviet Union; the French foreign minister; the commander in chief of NATO, General Nordstad; the secretary general of NATO, Spaak; the Duke and Duchess of Windsor; Alì Khan; Begum; millionaire Arthur Lopez; and the Rothschilds. The entertainment world included Juliette Greco, Matine Carol, Brigitte Bardot, Sacha Distel, Charlie Chaplin, and Françoise Sagan.

The millionaires present included Aristotle Onassis and his court. The Greek magnate was utterly struck by what he saw. Despite all his billions, he

would never have managed to attract such interest and bring so much attention to himself, not even amongst important politicians. This detail impressed him immensely. He probably thought: "If I had that woman by my side, I'd astonish the world."

So, a few days after the concert, Onassis telephoned Callas with all the kindness, admiration, and cordiality he had lacked in Venice the year before.

As 1959 began, Maria Callas travelled to America for a series of concerts

in St. Louis, Philadelphia, New York, and Washington. She returned to Italy at the end of spring and went to Venice for a party organized in her honor by Countess Castelbarco. Onassis was also there and was delighted to see her again; he greeted her and invited her to his luxury yacht *Christina*. He talked to Maria at length about his yacht, the famous people who sailed with him, and insisted that Maria and her husband accompany him on a cruise.

From Venice, Maria continued her artistic tour all over Europe: Madrid, Barcelona, Hamburg, Stockholm, Munich, Wiesbaden. At the end of May, Onassis telephoned from Monte Carlo to repeat his invitation and then travelled to London to see the first night of *Medea* at Covent Garden. To impress Maria, the magnate organized a party similar to the one held in Paris. He had invitations printed with the wording: 'Mr. & Mrs. Onassis take pleasure in inviting you to the party in honor of Maria Callas to be held at the Dorchester at 11:15 p.m. on Thursday, June 17.' On the evening of the debut, he set himself up in the bar to welcome his guests, offering tickets for the opera and glasses of champagne. He had managed to bring together an

impressive group: the Churchills (but not Sir Winston); the Duchess of Kent and her daughter, Princess Alexandra; the musician cousin of the Queen, Lord Harewood; actors Douglas Fairbanks and Gary Cooper. The party after the opera caused a great stir and the newspapers described it as the high-society event of the year.

Maria was not impressed by Onassis's attentions and shrugged him off every time they met. She was very aloof and cold that evening. She didn't even want to go to the party and Meneghini took great pains to convince her that they had to go. As soon as they arrived, Onassis dashed to embrace her but shortly after Maria said she was tired and was accompanied back to the hotel by her husband.

The performances of *Medea* went on until the end of June. Callas then gave concerts in Amsterdam and Brussels. She returned to her villa in Sirmione on July 15.

She was tired, exhausted. She called in her doctor again, who ordered her to go to the seaside. Meneghini organized a brief holiday at Venice Lido but at precisely the same time Onassis phoned yet again to invite Callas and her husband for a cruise on the *Christina* he was organizing for the second half of July.

"This invitation has come at just the right time," Meneghini said to his wife. "Your doctor has ordered seaside air. It would be absurd for the two of us to rent a yacht. Everyone says that this Greek's yacht is extremely comfortable. Let's give it a try. If you don't like it, we can leave at the first port and return home." Maria was perplexed. "It seemed she felt something threatening in the air," Meneghini was to confide later. But in the end, she let herself be convinced.

Departure from Monte Carlo was set for July 22. A week earlier, Maria and Meneghini moved to their house in Milan to prepare their luggage. Maria prepared complete outfits with swimwear and lingerie designed by Biki. Leaving Milan for Monte Carlo, she told the housekeeper: "Always keep the house ready. I may stay away a week or come back after a day. It depends on my companions."

Elsa Maxwell, who continued to be friends with Maria despite their argument some months earlier, knew about everything. She immediately wrote a letter to Callas which was delivered to her hotel in Monte Carlo. "Dear Maria, I am writing to wish you and Battista a splendid trip onboard that wonderful yacht in the company of that marvelous and intelligent host Ari, and that former statesman, sadly somewhat in decline today, who saved the world in 1940. As it happens, you will take the place of Garbo, by now too old, on the *Christina*. Good luck. I never liked Garbo and I

have loved you. From now on, enjoy every moment of your life. Take (and this is a delicate art) everything. Give (not a delicate art but important) everything you can allow yourself to give. This is the way towards true happiness, which you must discover in the desert of doubt."

Well-wishing words which seem to be the conclusion of a long and delicate task of mediation conducted behind the scenes. Words which also suggest how the new guest should behave onboard the *Christina*, by no means an occasional guest but one destined to take the

place of a legendary actress. It seemed as if Maria were being officially invested in her new role.

The *Christina* left the port of Monte Carlo at 2:00 a.m. on July 22. There were many important people onboard: Winston Churchill with his wife and

anchored in the Gulf of Corinth. Life on board was happy and relaxed. "The way these people behaved," wrote Meneghini in a kind of onboard diary, "was very different to what Maria and I were used to. We had the impression of being among a crowd of slightly crazy people. The majority of couples separated, finding other partners. Women and even men often sunbathed in the nude and were amorous in broad daylight in front of everyone. To put it bluntly, we had the impression of being in a huge pigsty."

The group made excursions in every port where the yacht anchored, at times on foot, at other times on donkeys. On August 4, the yacht anchored at Smirne, Onassis's birthplace. "That evening the Greek wanted to take me to dinner to meet his childhood friends," wrote Meneghini in his diary. "We visit-

"When you realized I was about to be overwhelmed, why didn't you do something?"

daughter, Diana; Lord Moran and the Montague Browns; Gianni Agnelli and his wife Marella; and many other Greek, American, and English personalities.

The first stop was Portofino, followed by Capri. The yacht sailed from the Mediterranean to the Aegean and

ed certain dives near the port and caroused with smugglers, prostitutes, and other unsavory characters until the morning. At 5:00 a.m. I managed to convince him to return to the yacht. He was so drunk he could hardly stand up."

On August 6, the yacht anchored in

front of Mount Athos and on August 7, the group was received by Patriarch Atenagora. The patriach knew both Onassis and Callas because they were two famous Greeks. He seemed honored by their presence and completely ignored the rest of the group, continuing to speak only with them in Greek. He seemed convinced that they were husband and wife and, at the end of the visit, wanted to bless them, as they stood next to each other in front of him. It almost appeared as if he conducted a wedding ceremony.

Maria was deeply disturbed by that

strange ritual. Sensitive to mysterious facts and the symbolic meaning of certain events, in that meeting with the head of the Orthodox Church she found almost a kind of hint of destiny.

It seemed that the blessing of the patriarch released an interior decision. From that moment, she abandoned herself to Aristotle Onassis. "That evening," wrote Meneghini in his diary, "I realized Maria had changed. She didn't want to go to bed early as usual. When I said I was tired and wanted to retire, she answered: 'Do what you want, I'm staying here.' The intrigue began that evening. I didn't immediately realize what was going on. She later accused me of not having done anything to save her. She said: 'When you realized I was about to be overwhelmed, why didn't you do something?' But I couldn't even dream for a minute that she was in trouble of such a kind."

Everything happened just like that, quite suddenly—as in a television soap opera. That overwhelming passion that, a few months later, the press would describe as "the love story of the centu-ry," filling magazine columns in half the world for years, happened and developed in the space of just a couple of hours. It was a bolt out of the blue, at least from the information we have gleaned.

Callas gave no direct accounts or versions of this passion. Maria never wanted to talk about it, even when the whole episode was over.

Meneghini, on the other hand, noted the daily developments in his diary. Finding himself unexpectedly in the middle of a reality he never could have imagined possible and which

broke his heart, Giovan Battista perhaps found a little comfort in confiding this earthquake of events and feelings to the pages of his diary. He wrote as if in a state of shock. Day after day, a few sentences, a few remarks and certain considerations.

Yet this diary is an important document. It is the firsthand account of an event which destroyed a fablelike marriage and stole from the world of opera its greatest talent of the century. It was an episode which ended a "golden period of fine singing" in the history of opera, a period which was to remain incomparable.

This document is now in our possession and we provide certain significant excerpts to illustrate what really happened.

August 7:
"Maria always dances with Onassis. She has let herself go like I've never seen before. I am almost happy about this. Maria is still a young woman, and if she enjoys herself it will do her good."

August 9:
"We're in Athens. We went to a reception in the evening and only returned at 4:00 a.m. Onassis and Maria always want parties on the yacht. 'I'm going to bed,' I tell her, and leave Maria with Onassis."

"You seem like my prison warden. You never leave me alone. In all these years, you have kept me chained up. I am tired of it all. You are not sporty. You can't speak languages. Your hair is never in place. You don't know how to dress elegantly."

August 10:
"This morning I woke up at 9:30 and realized Maria wasn't here. I looked for her all over the yacht. I met Onassis, smiling and happy. He told me he had slept and had a shave. An atrocious doubt flashed through my mind: 'If Onassis was asleep, where was Maria?' I went back to our cabin and Maria was there. She was distracted and in a strange mood. She began to talk about the beauty of the night and the fascination of dawn at sea. Then she became disrespectful and offensive, telling me that I should stop being her shadow. She said: 'You seem like my prison warden. You never leave me alone. In all these

years, you have kept me chained up. I am tired of it all. You are not sporty. You can't speak languages. Your hair is never in place. You don't know how to dress elegantly."

August 11:
"Last night I went to bed around midnight. Maria said to me: 'Go to bed, I'm staying here.' Around 2:00 a.m., I heard the door of the cabin open. I thought it was Maria but it wasn't my wife: it was Tina Onassis. Sobbing, she said to me: 'Battista, we're two sad souls. Your Maria is down in the lounge in the arms of my husband. There is nothing left to do, he's taken her from you.' Tina then left, leaving me in a dreadful state. Maria returned at 6:10 a.m. I asked her why she was so late, but she never replied."

August 13:
"I didn't see Maria at all yesterday. I went to bed early and passed a sleepless night. Maria came in at 5:15 a.m. By 2:00 p.m. we were in Monte Carlo, at 4:00 p.m. at Nice Airport and in Milan at 5:00 p.m. . . ." Maria said she preferred not to come to Sirmione. She wanted to spend the holiday in our house in Milan. However, she wants to be alone."

August 14:
"I went to bed at 2:00 this morning. Maria was sleeping soundly, her sleep seemed to be calm and peaceful. I got up at 5:00 and returned to the study to work. At 9:00 I was ready to leave for Sirmione and I went to our bedroom to say goodbye to Maria. She seemed affectionate but very distant. She suddenly asked me, point blank: 'What would you do if I no longer wanted to be with you?' I felt the blood rush to my head and everything spin around me. I smiled and said: 'I would retire to one of those rocky retreats where the monks live on Mount Athos.' I wanted to make Maria believe I thought her question a joke.

But I know my wife too well not to understand that she wasn't speaking off-hand. I sensed in all her behavior the immense storm that was about to engulf me. It was all over for me."

August 15:
"I phoned Maria at 8:00. She was surprised and upset because I hadn't phoned last night. I said 'I thought you were going to call me. Perhaps I misunderstood. Please forgive me.' She insisted again that she wanted to be alone in

Milan. 'I rest better,' she said. 'If there's anything new, I'll phone you.'"

At 12:15, Maria phoned and asked me to go immediately and see her in Milan. . . I dashed there with my heart in my throat. I arrived at 3:00, half an hour later than expected because of the holiday traffic. Maria asked to talk. . . She closed the doors so that the servants wouldn't hear anything and then confessed everything. She said, coldly: 'It's all over between us and I have decided to live with Onassis. . . He can't live without me and I can't live without him. . . He cares about you and thinks highly of you. . . He wants to see you to talk.' I listened as cold as a stone. I could think of nothing else to say but 'Tell him to come, I'll meet him with pleasure. I'll be strong, I can handle everything.'

"Onassis arrived at 10 in the evening. . . Neither of us could begin a conversation. I spoke first. . . 'Let's minimize the scandal,' I said. 'I will do what I can to help you in your plans, but understand what you are about to do,

128

the crime you are about to commit, the people you will kill'. . . Onassis tried to reassure me: 'Such things happen in life,' he said. I could kill him with my bare hands."

August 16:
"Last night's conversation went on until 3:00 in the morning. I was crushed when I went to bed. Maria stayed up with Onassis for another hour. When she came into the bedroom, I pretended to be asleep. She slipped into bed, in

anymore. I can't remember whether I had anything at all to eat today. I'm unsteady. I'm nervous. I think of Maria having dinner with Onassis in my home in Milan. Maria asked if they could eat there so they wouldn't be seen together around town. I said that it made no difference to me."

August 17:
". . . I told Maria I wanted to meet Onassis in an appropriate place. Maria called me back to ask if she could come

her place, and drowsed. I was shaking like a leaf. Perhaps I had a temperature.

"At 6:00 I got up and left my home without troubling anyone. I was crying as I went out of the door. I went to Zevio to see my mother, who kept on asking me 'How is Maria? Where is Maria? Why isn't Maria here?'

"I arrived in Sirmione at 6:00. It took me three hours to drive just over twenty miles. I feel I'm not connecting

with him. . . At 8:00 p.m., an enormous car drove through the gates of my villa in Sirmione. Maria, Onassis, our maid in Milan, and the two poodles, Toy and Tea, got out. . . Onassis was euphoric. He greeted everyone cordially, in a loud voice. His breath stank of alcohol. The driver told me he had drunk almost a whole bottle of whisky between Milan and Sirmione. He showed it to me. 'I bought it before we left,' he said. It was

Opposite page:

1958. Maria Callas in a photographic portrait by the famous English photographer Cecil Beaton. The portrait was made on Onassis's request. A friend of the photographer, Onassis told Beaton that he was enchanted with Callas and wanted a keepsake.

Side:

1959. Maria Callas with Tina Livanos, the wife of Onassis, during the cruise on the Christina. *In his memoirs, Meneghini wrote: "One night, I heard the door of the cabin open. I thought it was my wife but it was Tina, who said: 'We're two sad souls. Your Maria is down in the lounge in the arms of my husband.'"*

Above:

1957. Maria Callas, her husband, and American journalist Elsa Maxwell. It was Maxwell who introduced Onassis to Callas and insisted that the soprano accept the invitation to go on the famous cruise on the Christina *during which she fell in love with the Greek magnate.*

practically empty.

"Maria had also been drinking. I'd never seen her in such an altered state. . . After dinner, we went into the garden. . . Maria took Onassis up the little tower to admire the lake. . . Onassis said to me: 'You must have been mad to keep a woman like Maria cooped up on the shores of a puddle like this lake. . .' We retired to the lounge and began to talk. . . I was no longer as passive and stunned as before in Milan. Onassis accused me of wanting them to be unhappy, of being cruel. I lost my temper and attacked him. I offended him brutally. . . Maria began to tremble and cry convulsively. Onassis also began to cry. He said: 'I may be a swine, a murderer, a thief, pitiless, the most awful human being on this Earth, but I am also a billionaire and very powerful. I will never give Maria up, I will wrench her from anyone by whatever means, sending everyone, contracts and conventions to hell. . . How many millions do you want to give me Maria? Five? Ten?' I answered: 'You're just a poor drunkard and make me sick. I'd like to break your smug chin but I won't touch you because you can't even stand up. . .'

"Maria screamed hysterically, 'I was your ruin, I'll never be in peace again.' Onassis asked if we wanted to be alone: 'It's not necessary,' I answered. 'As far as I'm concerned, the conversation is over.'

"'So we can say goodbye?' said Onassis. 'I don't want to shake hands with a worm like you,' I answered. 'You invited me on to your blasted yacht and then you stabbed me in the back. I damn

you and hope you never have a minute's peace for the rest of your days.'

"I went up to my room. Maria made to follow me and then asked to be left awhile with Onassis. 'Do whatever you want,' I replied.

"I lay down fully dressed. At 4:00 in the morning, Maria tiptoed into the room. She took something to wear and left. I thought she would return later. I still had-

n't seen her by 5:00. I got up and went downstairs. There was no one around. Only our poodle Tea was sleeping in its usual place. Onassis's car was no longer in the courtyard. I went to Bruna's room,

"It's all over between us. I have decided to live with Onassis. . .

He can't live without me and I can't live without him. . .

He cares about you and thinks highly of you. . .

He wants to see you to talk."

but her bed was still made."

August 18:
"Maria phoned from Milan at 7:00 in the morning and told me she was at home.

Opposite page:

1959. In the early days of their relationship, Maria Callas and Onassis were continually hounded by photographers. In this photo, they pretend to go separate ways.

Center:

1960. Maria Callas and Onassis posing for photographers now that their relationship is in the open and there was nothing left to hide.

Below: 1959. A close-up of Maria Callas at the time she was falling in love with Onassis.

She asked me to send our servant Ferruccio with her passport, our 'little Madonna', a small 1500s painting I had given her on the day we met which had seen us through twelve years of struggles, bitterness, tears, hopes, and joys. "She told me she wanted to accept my proposal, to finish everything quickly with a clean, neat cut, saving herself as much as possible from shame and ignominy. I advised her to think again. What would come, would come.

"I phoned my mother in Zevio at 9:00. At 10:00 I phoned conductor Nicola Recigno but I didn't know what to say to him and asked him to call me back. Walter Legge phoned from London at 11:00. They phoned from Copenhagen at midday. The whole opera world continued to contact me about Maria's engagements without the slightest idea of the tragedy which had overtaken us."

August 19:
"Maria telephoned after midday to confirm the separation and asked that proceedings begin immediately. She wanted all the accounts, she wanted to know everything. 'I want my complete freedom,' she said and told me not to bother her with letters or supplications."

August 22:
"I went to Turin and spent the whole day examining documents with the lawyer. I arrived home in Milan at 7:00 in the evening. The maid said Maria had left the evening before with some friends. She wrote a note with her address: Hotel Hermitage, Monte Carlo. I had something to eat and went to rest.

Maria phoned at 9:00. She said she was well and happy. Newspaper *Stampa Sera* published a brief piece saying that Callas had been seen passing through Cuneo in the company of Onassis."

August 23:
"I worked all day sorting out papers and documents. My accountant came round about noon. I told him what was happening and he was horrified. Nobody phoned all day. I picked up the phone a few times but it was dead. I thought about the storms the day before and bombarded the phone company with protests. I finally found out, from a clerk who at least gave me his name, that my telephone had been cut off following 'a request for termination of the contract.' Who could ever have played such a

trick on me? I took the train to Sirmione at 8:00. I am now in my study, working. I feel so frighteningly sad without Maria."

August 24:
"No calls, no communications. I went to see my mother. When I came home, the maid said my wife had phoned twice. She was tired and had gone to bed, asking me to call tomorrow at 11:00."

August 25:
"I spoke to Maria at 11:00. She said she wanted my peace and well-being in the future. She let it be understood she wanted the house in Milan. She asked: 'Will you also give me the jewels.' 'We'll have to talk about it,' I answered."

August 26:
"Maria phoned and asked that Emma send her all toiletries, lingerie, and clothes. She asked insistently that I return all Elsa Maxwell's letters. She begged me to do everything quickly

and close the whole matter as soon as possible.

"'Ask all saints "why?",' she said. 'I need peace.' 'I need peace and quiet, as well,' I said. 'You ruined my life. You can be grateful to be in such good health at your age,' she said. 'You have lived your life and should be prepared to stand aside. I've been with you for twelve years. Enough is enough. I have the right to change things.'

"I answered that when we got married, there were no conditions or expiration dates. Our pacts were different then. I also reminded her how, in the last few years, she insisted continually that I should buy a tomb in Sirmione Cemetery so that we could be together even after death. 'After the villa you have bought for my old age,' she once said, 'I want you to buy a place where we can be together when we have passed from this life.'

"This annoyed her. She got angry. She said she felt she was right. 'I didn't want nor did I look for this situation,'

she said. 'If it happened, it was destiny. I want a definitive and honest settlement in my life.' 'Go and ask all your saints advice to find out whether you are right,' I answered. 'Go to that Madonna in Milan Cathedral where we bent our knees and implored all those times. What have you done, Maria, of all our promises? All our vows? All our prayers? All our work? You have turned it all into a nameless shame!'"

August 27:
No telephone calls today. In the afternoon, I went to Zevio to see my mother. She has intuitively understood what is happening. She won't live much longer, is very sad, and is once again obliged to feel the despair of a new disgrace in our family. My poor mother."

August 28:
With the lawyer in Turin. I told him my idea to take my wife and Onassis to court. He dissuaded me because Maria is American and could not be incrimi-

nated. Maria phoned while I was with the lawyer. She was not in Milan but Nice. In the evening, I went to my home in Milan and stopped there to work for a couple of hours. I saw that Maria had left without taking the little picture of the 'Madonnina.' She always used to take it with her. I asked Bruna for an explanation and she said: 'By now, that

me to go to Milan so she could be free to go out with Onassis.'"

September 6:
"The news broke in Verona. The local press picked up the gossip around town. The journalists arrived. I tried to keep everything quiet but they didn't believe a word I said."

picture doesn't mean anything to Maria.'"

August 30:
"The newspapers had the first news of the row between me and Maria. Nothing specific. Maria is in Monte Carlo."

September 3:
"Bruna phoned to say that Maria wasn't very well and asked me to put off my trip

September 7:
The Milan afternoon newspaper *La Notte* fired the first shot, followed by all the other newspapers. Everyone now knows about the whole business."

September 10:
"Maria has disappeared together with Onassis. The journalists are hounding me. I'm tired, I gave an interview and let myself go; it received prominent cover-

"Watch out, Battista: One day or another
I will come to Sirmione with a gun and kill you."

to Milan for a few days because she wanted to be calm. 'As she wishes,' I said."

September 4:
"I went to the lawyer in Turin. At the motorway exit I saw the front page of the afternoon newspaper with a headline about Callas meeting Onassis. Unwell my foot. My wife did not want

age. Maria was told about it. She phoned me from London, furious. She criticized me harshly. I lost my temper and exploded. She threatened me. She said: 'Watch out, Battista: One day or another I will come to Sirmione with a gun and kill you.' 'Come by all means,' I answered, raving mad. 'I'll have a machine gun.' It's the end, violent and

"You've lived your life by now. You should be prepared to stand aside. I've been with you for twelve years. That's more than enough."

beyond repair."

Callas's behavior throughout the whole affair, right from the start, seemed very strange. A year before, she said: "A man can never change completely but a woman can." Were the experiences of the last few years changing her character and approach to life? As already mentioned, it almost seemed as if she had prepared the break, perhaps even with the cooperation of Elsa Maxwell. The letter which the gossip columnist wrote just before the cruise is very significant. "From now on, enjoy every moment of your life." Arianna Stassinopoulos, who has investigated this topic, gleaned the following statement from Peter Diamand, director of the Holland Festival. Ten days before the cruise on the *Christina*, Callas gave some concerts in Amsterdam. At a reception after one of the concerts, she said to Diamand: "I'd like to talk to you privately, just the two of us without Battista." They met the next day and Maria asked Peter not to pay her fee into the joint Callas-Meneghini account. "Hang on to the money until I give new instructions," she said, "I'll be in touch. There are going to be changes in my life, over the next few months. That's what my instinct tells me. . . You will soon hear something quite new. . . Show me that you are a friend." "Maria, how melodramatic!" replied Peter Diamand. "No, it's not melodramatic," she answered, "let's just say it's dramatic." What did she mean by all this?

When the news of her relationship with Onassis hit the newspapers, Maria made a statement in which she claimed that her marriage had been in trouble for some time. "I confirm that the separation between me and my husband is definitive and complete. The decision has been in the air for some time and the cruise on the *Christina* was pure coincidence. Our lawyers are handling matters and will soon make their own statements. I am now my own manager. In these extremely painful personal circumstances, I ask everyone to be understanding. . . Mr. Onassis and I have been very close friends for some time. I even have a professional relationship with him. I have been asked to sing at the Monte Carlo Opera and there is even talk of a film."

Was all this true? Or was it merely an attempt to justify a very hasty decision? Meneghini always denied that

there were problems between him and his wife prior to the cruise on the *Christina*. He even wrote: "Everyone onboard Onassis's yacht realized how much we were in love. We were laughed at for our sense of reserve and our romantic behavior."

In the meantime, the newspapers continued to madly pursue the story. Onassis was followed everywhere by photographers. The paparazzi caught him on several occasions leaving hotels or restaurants with Callas and the photos inevitably appeared in magazines. *Time*, under the headline "Love and Money," told the story in ironic form giving everyone opera roles: Maria Meneghini Callas, a famous star, was the

magnate, tenor; Tina Onassis, his young and beautiful wife, mezzo-soprano.

Maria in the meantime had resumed her singing. In Milan, she recorded *La Gioconda* for EMI-His Master's Voice. She then continued the series of concerts begun prior to the cruise on the *Christina*: She sang in Bilbao, London, Berlin, Kansas City, and, in November, performed two operas in Dallas.

This was followed by a long hiatus, almost a year off the stage. The world of opera was displeased that Callas had left her husband, and theater superintendents were reluctant to negotiate and sign contracts with the mistress of one of the richest men in the world. Having

soprano; Giovan Battista Meneghini, her aged husband, was the bass; Elsa Maxwell, her confidante, baritone; Evangelia Callas, the neglected mother, contralto; Aristotle Onassis, wealthy

completed the engagements already organized by Battista Meneghini, Callas found herself out of work.

Callas also had serious problems with her voice in this period. "I must

"I confirm that the separation between me and my husband is definitive and complete. The decision has been in the air for some time and the cruise on the Christina was pure coincidence. Our lawyers are handling matters and will soon make their own statements. I am now my own manager. In these extremely painful personal circumstances, I ask everyone to be understanding. . ."

admit," she wrote in a long note, "that I had terrible problems with my singing. I had awful problems with my right jawbone but nonetheless continued singing so that people couldn't claim I cancelled concerts. Moreover, the newspapers continued frequently to write that I had lost my voice, to the point that I began to believe them. I began saying to myself that it had to be true if that was what everyone was saying. I had a hernia near the appendix which affected my stomach muscles and shortened my stamina, as well as troubling my whole singing; the abdomen and diaphragm are just as important as the vocal cords. For the first time ever, I submitted to these difficulties and lost all my audacity. Thank God my vocal cords have always been in perfect shape. It is an exaggeration to say they are ruined. But this negative criticism caused me such anxiety that even I thought I had problems with my voice.

"On top of this, as I have already said, my nasal cavity was clogged with fluid and I lost all my resonance. I then began to stretch my voice. When the fluid moved to the vocal cords and prevented all possible resonance, it was like a deaf man shouting, since I could no longer hear myself."

Permanent vocal damage seemed imminent to Maria. Losing her voice would mean losing her status, becoming just another ordinary woman, a former star. Perhaps this prospect disrupted her sleep and influenced the decisions in her private life. Because of her art, she had become the most famous woman in the world. And perhaps she thought that having a husband as rich and powerful as Onassis would have meant she could still be "the divine," "the queen of opera," even if she no longer sang, even if her voice was not what it once was.

But the reactions of the public proved her wrong. She realized, immediately after her separation from Meneghini, that people, those who had always loved her, were losing interest. This caused her great bitterness, since the affection and admiration of her fans were her lifeblood. Behaving like a child, she tried to blame everything on her husband, denying everything she had declared in public beforehand. In an autobiographical burst of anger, she wrote: "The world has condemned me for leaving my husband. But I didn't leave him. He left me because I no longer wanted him to handle my affairs.

"Battista himself said that our marriage would have been pointless unless he could have complete authority over me. I think this was the only thing he wanted. I didn't want to marry an impresario. If that was what I'd wanted, I would at least have married a professional. "Battista always complained about my every caprice, about every expression of my temperament. It was he who was always intransigent with opera houses in order to attain higher fees. He claimed that I was immovable. Naturally enough, I wanted to be paid for what I thought I was worth. But I was never obsessed with money, especially when discussing an important performance or a major venue. . . I know that people say I am avaricious. I would

137

just call myself far-sighted. I have always been afraid of having to live my old age in poverty or even die poverty-stricken."

These were ineffective outbursts. Nobody believed what she said anymore. And Callas, in an attempt to justify herself, attacked her former husband even more. "My husband kept me caged up for so long that the day I met Aristo and his friends, so full of life and vitality, I felt like another woman. Living with a man so much older than I, I became prematurely depressed and old. I got fat, like Battista. I couldn't think of anything other than money and my reputation. Now, at last, I am an ordinary woman. Happy. Even if I have to admit that life for me began at forty, or thereabouts. . ."

These are weighty statements but in complete contrast with the letters, notes, and affectionate outpourings Maria continued to write to her husband until shortly before the cruise. Meneghini racked his brains to find a valid reason for this sudden and total change. He became angry on reading the statements

of his ex-wife. "I created Maria Callas and she repaid me with a stab in the back," he said to journalists. "When I met her, she was fat, clumsy, dressed like a dog, a real gypsy. She didn't have a cent and didn't have the least prospect of making a career for herself. I had to pay her hotel room and give her seventy dollars so that she could remain in Italy. And now, from what I hear, I'm accused of having exploited her."

Their great love story finished in the gossip columns, with harsh words, revenge, and vendetta. Maria wanted a divorce because she hoped to marry Onassis, but Meneghini had no intention of granting it. The situation was far from rosy for Callas. "I'm in an awful situation because of Italian law," she wrote. "I can't be truly free because Battista keeps check on me all the time. I daren't be photographed alone with a good friend because he would claim the relationship is ostentatious. I daren't be photographed in public in Paris with the same man for three nights running.

"If I married tomorrow and had a child—and like every woman I want to have many children—by Italian law I would be imprisoned for two years. I'm not sure if I will still think about remarrying, if I should ever be free to do so. Once married, men think everything is owed to them. And I don't like people telling me what to do. My instinct and

my convictions tell me what I should or should not do. These convictions may or may not be right, but they are mine. And I have the courage of my convictions. People can say what they want. It is very easy to gossip about other people. I don't believe in compromises. Especially when they involve me and my life."

Despite these statements, marrying Onassis was the goal Maria wanted to achieve at all costs, not the least because she knew that it was only in this way that she could, to some extent, "justify" the breakup with Meneghini in the eyes of the world. Her dream, however, lasted less than a year. In 1960, Onassis separated from his wife, Tina. Maria was happy and thought the time had come to put her relationship with the shipping magnate in order. One evening, while she was at Maona, the most fashionable place in Monte Carlo nightlife, she let slip to journalists that she soon hoped to marry. Yet when Onassis read these comments in the newspapers, he immediately denied the fact. "It's all imagination," he said, "Maria was only joking." Clear, dry words. Callas realized that perhaps her secret dream would never come true.

Furthermore, Onassis—to make it clear she should have no illusions—began to show the true side of his character more and more openly: He was coarse, egotistical, intransigent, a chauvinist, and vulgar. When he first met her, he planned great things with her, saying they would go into business together. They had even talked about a great opera company to be set up in Monte Carlo. But as time passed, there was less and less talk of business. After a year living with Onassis, Maria had become the magnate's slave. She no longer received the attentions that he initially showered upon her. She felt

the audience, but Onassis did not turn up. Maria was widely adulated that evening: Twenty thousand people deliriously applauded her onstage with as many as seventeen curtain calls.

In December of the same year, while she was performing *Medea* at La Scala in Milan, she went to the hospital for a painful operation on her nasal cavity. She remained in the hospital alone: Aristotle Onassis never once visited her.

Onassis's absence from Maria's

neglected, unappreciated, and she was often humiliated by Onassis in public.

In August 1960, she returned to sing in Greece, in the ancient Herodus Atticus Amphitheater. She performed *Norma*, the opera she loved the most, and received a glorious welcome from her countrymen. In 1961, she returned again, performing *Medea*, a Greek heroine in ancient myths immortalized by the great Greek playwrights. It was an occasion of extremely fascinating cultural content, which Maria was particularly anxious to perform. She would have wanted the man she loved at her side, a Greek like her and much anticipated by

important engagements became more frequent and more apparent. Onassis often travelled the world for weeks without ever letting Callas know where he was. To be with him, she was forced to go to places quite unsuited to her own tastes: yachts and nightclubs. One evening, in a nightclub, she heard the show announced: "And here tonight, ladies and gentlemen, the Callas of striptease." Onassis giggled amusedly. She blushed with shame and left on her own.

She began to realize that she had made a mistake once again. She had sacrificed her entire world for Onassis but

Opposite page, bottom:

Maria Callas in a close-up taken in Barcelona where she gave a concert at the Liceum Theater.

Opposite page, top:

1960. Maria Callas during the performance of Norma at the Epidaurus Theater before retrieving a bunch of flowers thrown on stage by the audience. These performances were memorable. The theater was filled every evening with 15,000 people from all over Greece.

Side:

1960. Maria Callas with her father George, who saw her performances of Norma in Greece.

Above:

1959. Maria Callas in an affectionate pose with a young girl. The soprano always wanted children, first with Meneghini and later with Onassis, but was never so fortunate.

he had not kept any of the promises he had made. When he had guests, he enjoyed humiliating her. "Who are

"By now I am at the mercy of this man. He was everything to me.

The dream which I hoped would crown my life. But it has finished badly."

you?" he asked. "You're nobody. You are a woman with a whistle in her throat that doesn't work anymore."

impressions were not based in reality.

"Onassis treated her really badly. I witnessed several incredible scenes. I even had a violent argument with the man to defend Maria. One evening, during a dinner on the *Christina*, after one

her, hoped she would bear his child. She knew that, given her age, the idea of pregnancy was rather dangerous. But she tried anyway. She became pregnant. But the problems started immediately and a miscarriage was increasingly likely. She thought of going to a famous Swiss clinic, but she lost the child after four months.

"Maria, in the early days of her relationship with Onassis, often said: 'I'm finished with opera. I am utterly fed up

with sacrifices, stressful rehearsals, and exhausting performances. I want to retire and rest for a while. Then I will give a performance every now and then.'"

When she realized that the idyll with Onassis wasn't working, she tried to get back into the world of music. But it was too late. And, especially, in the wake of the constant humiliations she received from Onassis, she no longer had the determination and audacity of the early years.

"I never ceased telling her that she should resume her career, and, only by becoming a great singer again, free herself of the man. She said I was right. At one point, she decided to put my advice into action. But Onassis did everything possible to obstruct her, since he knew that, through her art, Callas would be able to overcome his arrogance.

"Early in 1964, I managed to get her back into an opera theater, to perform *Tosca* at Covent Garden in London. Through sacrifices and hard work in rehearsals, she was in splendid physical and vocal form. She was amazingly successful, just like the old times. That triumph soothed the sadnesses which gnawed away at her private life. It could have been the onset of a great return. That was why I mentioned my old project again—have her perform *Tosca* in an operatic film. Thanks to her stage

Zeffirelli, who was still her friend, often tried to defend her. He told us: "I am increasingly convinced that Onassis never loved Maria. He was an untrustworthy man. I always felt something false when I was with him. At the beginning of her relationship with him, I confided these impressions to Maria but she answered: 'Can't you see? He adores me, he can't live without me.' She was convinced of the love of that man, but as time passed she realized that her

of these scenes, Maria, red in face from yet another humiliation and with tears in her eyes, got up, and went to her cabin. I went to her. 'Why don't you leave him and sing again?' I asked her. She answered: 'How can I? By now I am at the mercy of this man. He was everything to me. The dream which I hoped would crown my life. But it has finished badly.'"

Onassis adored his children, and Maria, in an attempt to make him marry

Opposite page, left:

1959. A photo of Maria Callas at the time of her separation from Meneghini. Despite the feelings which had bonded her to her husband, she was extremely determined to get a divorce as quickly as possible. On August 5, 1959, she told Meneghini: "It's all over between us and I have decided to live with Onassis. . . He can't live without me and I can't live without him. . ."

Opposite page, right:

Maria Callas (right) during a performance in Barcelona receiving a visit from Elvira De Hidalgo, the famous singer who had been her teacher in Greece 1939-1945.

Side: 1957. Maria Callas, wearing the very expensive costume of an Egyptian queen for the masked ball at the Waldorf Astoria in New York. On that occasion, Maria wore the jewels of the Harry Wilson collection, then worth more than a million dollars.

success, I was finally able to convince her. I had organized everything: producers, settings, operators. There was a meeting on the *Christina* to settle the final details before signing the contract. Onassis realized that Maria was escaping from his clutches and that the contract would have relaunched her on the world artistic scene, returning her dignity and strength. He thus began his maneuvers and, with diabolical shrewdness, convinced Maria to delegate him

to finalize the contract. Everything went up in smoke, as he had planned."

Already a year earlier, in 1963, Onassis had begun to take an interest in the Kennedys. He was fascinated by the speed with which the family had scaled the heights of power in America. He began to make projections and calculations, hoping to insinuate himself into their intriguing lives. Firstly, he began to court Princess Lee Radziwill, Jackie Kennedy's sister. He hoped to introduce himself through her to the most powerful family in America. But, after the tragic assassination of the president in Dallas on November 22, 1963, he made moves directly to his widow.

In the summer of 1963, while John Kennedy was still alive, Onassis met Jackie and managed to invite her on a cruise around the Greek archipelago on the *Christina*. After the death of the president, Onassis continued to telephone her and went to see her in New York. Maria knew all about this and suffered terribly, but put up with events, convinced in her heart that things would work out. But Onassis ignored her more and more and courted Jackie Kennedy more frequently and more openly.

In May 1968, Jackie Kennedy joined the *Christina* for a cruise in the Caribbean. Maria stayed at home. She was furious not only because Jackie was on the cruise but also because Onassis had given her the "Ithaca Suite," the

apartment reserved for guests of honor, where Winston Churchill had once stayed and which Maria herself had used in the past.

At the end of the cruise, the gossip was that Jackie Kennedy was seriously considering marrying again, with Onassis, but on June 6, Bobby Kennedy was assassinated and the gossip ceased. Maria thought it was mere talk, but her illusion was to last only a few weeks.

At the beginning of August, while on the *Christina*, Onassis told her: "You must return immediately to Paris. I'm being visited by the Kennedys and our awkward situation might embarrass them." Maria understood and replied:

Greece.

Maria was utterly depressed. She could find no peace anywhere. She felt that her adventure with Onassis was truly over and that, with this adventure, her life was finished as well. She left Paris and went to Dallas, then to Las Vegas and Los Angeles and, finally, to New York. It was in New York, one day in October, that she learned of the imminent marriage of Onassis and Jackie Kennedy.

"On the evening of October 16," Renata Tebaldi said, "I was to debut at the Metropolitan with Cilea's *Adriana Lecouvreur* and Maria Callas asked to see me. When they told me, I was quite

"For the first time ever, I submitted to these difficulties and lost all my audacity. Thank God my vocal cords have always been in perfect shape. It is an exaggeration to say they are ruined. But this negative criticism caused me such anxiety that even I thought I had problems with my voice."

"You will never see me again." She immediately packed her bags.

She returned to Paris. She learned from the newspapers that Teddy Kennedy, now the head of the family after the death of Bobby, was with Jackie on the *Christina* taking a cruise around

taken aback. I had been her historic rival and we had not spoken since 1949: Why did she want to see me? At the end of the opera, she came to my dressing room. When we stood in front of each other and looked into each other's eyes, we embraced. Maria embraced me tight-

142

ly and I could feel her shaking like a leaf. I felt her tears fall from her eyes onto my neck. I couldn't understand why she was so emotional. I understood everything the next day, reading the newspapers with the news that Onassis had decided to marry Jackie Kennedy. Callas had found out the day before. She was experiencing such dramatic human emotions that she had come to see me to release herself, since I represented the world she had sacrificed for the love of Onassis."

Onassis married Jackie Kennedy on October 20, 1968. The ceremony was held in the afternoon in the small chapel of Panaytsa, on the island of Skorpios. That chapel was Maria's favorite place, where she loved to remain alone, think, and pray, as she often did, especially in times of sadness and loneliness. She had the impression that the place was somehow "hers" and

suffered tremendously from the fact that Onassis had chosen it for his wedding.

Maria spent the day in her apartment on Avenue Georges Mandel in Paris. The telephone rang continuously but she did not want to speak to anyone. The servants were ordered to say that she was not at home. In the evening, she dressed to the nines and went to the first night of *Pulce nell'Orecchio*, adapted from Feydeau's work. She then went to celebrate the seventieth anniversary of Chez Maxim's, the famous Parisian restaurant.

Solitud
Last

"I am so fragile, behind my so-called self-control. . . I still have a long life to live and I must be worthy of all the gifts that have been given to me."

These two thoughts, which Maria wrote in a letter to a friend in October 1968, a few days after Onassis and Jackie Kennedy married, are the central theme of the last period of her life, the "post-Onassis" years, from October 1968 to September 16, 1977, the day she died.

In these words, Maria reveals all her despair. She, the iron woman who had fought colossal battles with theaters all over the world, triumphing over all her enemies and all her difficulties, felt fragile, finished, reduced to nothing, to the extent of even being "frightened to live." This is the real meaning of "I still have a long life to live. . ." Maria had thought about matters and realized that, since she was not yet forty-five, she could presume that she would live for

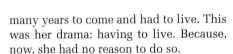

many years to come and had to live. This was her drama: having to live. Because, now, she had no reason to do so.

Onassis had killed her. By deciding to marry Jackie Kennedy, he had struck her a mortal blow. This is not rhetoric. From her childhood, Callas had always a specific objective: to become a great singer. To achieve this goal she had struggled, fought, and suffered more than can be imagined. When the dream of her life was at its peak of triumph, she had sacrificed it for something she felt was even more important: her love for Aristotle Onassis. Now, in repudiating her to marry another woman, Onassis had made her entire life "vain." And she, at forty-five, no longer had the desire or the enthusiasm to start again from scratch.

Having lived, as we have seen, the day of Onassis's wedding with immense pride, showing herself to the world in combative form, she fell prey to a more mortal interior state of confusion. She locked herself in her Paris apartment. The few people who were able to see her remarked that she was almost always in bed, slumbering with sleeping pills and pain-killers. "I've got a terrible migraine," she would say. In truth, she was trying to kill the pain of the stab to her heart.

But, life is life. And to live, we need reasons to live. Her two reasons for living had been singing and love. She had lost both but something had to be done

to find them again. She decided to try. The nine years which followed saw a series of failures until, at the end, Maria simply said, "Enough," and let herself die.

The pain Callas experienced when Onassis married is documented by a series of extraordinary confessions the soprano made to a very dear friend, American musicologist John Ardoin, which Arriana Stassinopoulos refers to extensively in her magnificent biography *Callas Beyond the Legend*.

Maria rarely complained, rarely confided her worries, and never her deepest pains. But to John Ardoin, whose professional seriousness and great humanity inspired Maria's trust, she opened her heart. Precisely at the time of her greatest sadness, she confided everything to him, even agreeing that the conversation could be recorded: "Nine years of retired life, of humiliated life, stay with you, can't be forgotten in just two months. . . A serious person, a person of character who promises and ensures you relative happiness should always keep his word. . . It's too easy to say, 'Well, you know how it is. . . I mean to say. . . We did everything possible to be happy! Well, thank you very much for these nine years.' And what am I left with? Not even a friendship. We can't be

friends, seeing how everything has worked out. How could he be my friend? Having humiliated me like that! It is easy to say that bitterness doesn't help. Sure, Christians would say that, I've read it in certain books. They'd say 'You should forget,' that 'You shouldn't

be bitter.' No, I'm not bitter, I'm in pain. . . After nine years, not even a child, not even a family, not even a friend! And so you ask yourself: 'Why, why? Why do such things happen?' Not the least because, in my silly logic, I am given to believe that if a person has had the privilege of winning a fine reputation, that person also has the right to be happy... It takes little to make me happy, but when you are dumped without even a thank you, it hurts, don't you think? You have a girlfriend and you care about her. Today she says she will love you forever and the day after, just like that, you treat her worse than a dog. It's a slap in the face. And if things always work out like this, they reduce you to a nervous wreck. . . Am I or am I not right? What hopes could I still have? For nine years, I waited for the best, but instead. . . How can a man be so dishonest?. . . I don't like losing. Who does? Frankly, the idea

of going home fills me with terror. I feel like I am living a nightmare. . . I'm terrified. . . I try anything to survive. . . There's no point in cultivating illusions: Happiness has no part in my destiny."

These are dramatic words, pronounced almost coldly, applying a piti-less logic towards herself which highlights the problem in all its desolation. Maria paints a terrible picture of the reality in which she found herself and asks herself desperate questions.

Later, she wrote in a letter to John Ardoin: ". . . Thank you for having been such a kind friend to me, so close and affectionate. You can't imagine how much strength you gave me. May God repay you for the affection and esteem you gave me. I returned exhausted. Too much emotion, I imagine."

And some time later, once these emotions had settled so that she could look to the future: ". . . So many things have happened, and, frankly, I can say that on the outside I am reacting well. But I am prey to extreme tension and try desperately to keep control. Naturally, I think it's a liberation but there is little faith left in me. At certain times, I feel calm and hopeful, at others I am utterly down. I fight against despair because it is un-Christian and undignified. In any case, my feelings are essentially pure. But what a solitary life awaits me, John! I will never be able to sing as well as in the past, nor can I expect to meet a man up to my hopes and standards (and I don't mean financially). Is it perhaps too

She began to consider various proposals for work, which arrived every now and then. In February and March of 1969, she recorded a concert conducted by Nicola Recigno. In the meantime, she even considered the possibility of returning to the stage. Luchino Visconti proposed an idea for a new staging of *La*

much to ask a person to be honest, loyal, faithful, passionate (on average, I mean)? I am very discouraged: I trust myself but I can't trust anyone from the past, present, or future. Perhaps I am strange? Forgive me this rather odd let-

Traviata for the Paris Opera and a film about the life of Giacomo Puccini. Joseph Losey wanted her to be the leading character in a film adapted from *Boom!* by Tennessee Williams. Pier Paolo Pasolini also contacted her, with a

"What a solitary life awaits me! I will never be able to sing as well as in the past, nor can I expect to meet a man up to my hopes and standards. . . Is it perhaps too much to ask a person to be honest, loyal, faithful, passionate? I am very discouraged: I trust myself but I can't trust anyone from the past, present, or future."

ter but I am living a very odd period."

Maria was alone. Perhaps she thought that work might have helped her forget. She was aware that it would be difficult to recuperate lost time, but she wanted to try. "I only need three years. . . Three years to become myself again. It is the beginning that frightens me. . . Yes, the beginning is terrible."

film project inspired by *Medea*. This was not to be a film of the tragedy by Euripides, nor even the operatic film of Cherubini's masterpiece, but a poetic interpretation of the myth of Medea. Maria accepted this proposal. "When Pasolini and Franco Rossellini, the producer of the film, gave me their proposal," she said later, "I didn't hesistate. I

147

understood that it was the occasion I had been waiting for and decided not to let it slip from my grasp."

Pasolini's film was an anchor of salvation for Callas. It was not only an excellent opportunity to be in the news again and return to the world of entertainment in an astonishing and immediate manner (an opera as such, as she herself wrote, would have taken three years of study), but it was an undertaking which would have distracted her from all her other worries. From this point of view, it was a fine dose of medicine.

Pasolini was enthusiastic. "We are in the presence of an artist who, in a certain sense, is the most modern of

able to work again had galvanized her and she was up at dawn every morning, although it was her usual everyday custom to sleep until noon. She had found, at least for the time being, a reason to live.

Callas always hated the Communists and had harsh words to say against Marxism on several occasions. She never forgot that it was the "Reds" who had forced her to leave Greece in 1945. But, with Pasolini, she forgot everything. To some extent, she even shared his way of looking at society through a Marxist philosophy imbued with Catholicism. When Pasolini commenced discussions of this kind, Maria listened to him enchantedly, fascinatedly. She

We are in a position to reconstruct the episode to the smallest detail, through the words of a major artist, painter Giuseppe Zigaina, who was also, to some extent, involved in the story.

"Maria fell hopelessly in love with Pier Paolo and dreamed of marrying him," we were told by Zigaina, Pasolini's brotherly friend who worked with him on several films, including *Medea.* "She confessed it to me herself, in tears, towards the end of filming, asking me to help her achieve her goal. I found myself in a very complicated situation, since it was well-known that Pier Paolo was homosexual, and it was by no means easy for me to act delicately, without hurting the feelings of one or

women," he declared. "However, an ancient creature lives inside her, strange, mysterious, arcane, hiding terrible interior conflicts. I am perfectly aware of her professional skills but they

quickly became fond of Pasolini and, naive to the limit of credibility, even fell in love with him.

Pasolini was kind, affectionate, and very attentive. Maria, thirsting for love,

the other.

"Pasolini had entrusted Callas to me so that I could look after her for the duration of filming. Every morning, I accompanied her in my little nine-meter boat from her hotel in Grado to the set, on a deserted island four miles away. The trip took an hour and a half, just the two of us. Callas preferred to prepare her make-up and costumes in the hotel. I took her back to Grado in the evening. We became friends. I was the only person with whom she spent so much time. She had a great need to open her heart, talk and find someone who would listen to her.

"When Pasolini and Franco Rossellini gave me their proposal for Medea, I didn't hesitate. I understood that it was the occasion I had been waiting for and decided not to let it slip from my grasp."

matter little to me. It was her human individuality that convinced me Callas could be my Medea."

The film involved very little dialogue. Maria had only to sing an old Greek nursery rhyme. The joy of being

was enthralled by his behavior and hopes and illusions began to re-emerge in her heart.

This is an extremely important fact in understanding the real Maria Callas. It reveals an incredibly ingenuous soul.

"I had first met her in March 1948, when she sang in Udine. I remembered her as being surprisingly overweight. Yet, in Grado, I found myself in the

company of a very fascinating, beautiful woman with jet-black eyes. An exceptional woman. Onassis had left her almost two years beforehand. She felt very lonely and was desperate for love. It was easy to perceive this—her anxiety was so evident.

"I noticed almost immediately that she was very fond of Pier Paolo. I thought that she was probably fascinated by his intelligence. Pasolini, when he wanted to, could enchant anyone. During our boat trips, she began asking me questions about Pasolini. When she found out how well I knew him, perhaps better than any other person, she spoke of nothing else. She wanted to know everything about him, even the most insignificant things. She asked me what he was like as a boy, when we had

met, how he lived, what he ate, what he thought, and even information about his mother, father, and brother who was killed during the Resistance. She wanted to know everything and listened with an interest and avidity which marveled me.

"It was the unmistakable behavior of a woman in love, but I would never have thought even for a moment that Callas had really fallen in love with Pier Paolo. Everyone knew that he wasn't attracted to women. Nino Davoli was also on the set, with whom Pier Paolo lived, and everyone knew about their relationship. I therefore assumed that Callas also knew how things stood. But, quite the opposite, she didn't know anything. As I discovered later, Callas was incredibly naive over the whole matter.

She saw that Pier Paolo was kind to her, concerned, gallant, and she mistook these attentions, an essential aspect of the amiable and sensitive nature of Pier Paolo, as signs of great love.

"Pier Paolo realized what was happening but even he did not think that things would take such a serious turn. Perhaps he even kept up the game so that Maria would not get bored. There are photographs of them kissing—Maria is kissing him on the mouth, just like a woman overwhelmed with passion, whereas he, if you look carefully, has his eyes wide open as if he were kissing a dummy.

"Pasolini was also a fine painter. He had painted some very valuable pictures when young. He dropped painting later to dedicate himself to literature and the

cinema. But every now and then, he liked to draw. As soon as he met Callas, he drew some magnificent portraits. I own them. . . Callas appears as a true, authentic, triumphant, alive, lofty person. You can see that he was greatly interested in her and very affectionate. But the following year, as filming was coming to an end, Pier Paolo's interest in Callas was changing. The portraits he continued to draw are different. Using large sheets of paper, he drew a series of profiles of Maria and then sprinkled drops of wine, rose petals or crushed poppies, squeezed grapes or coffee over the portraits. He then folded the sheet several times, pressed it and, on re-opening it, all the profiles had taken on an unusual coloring. But after a few hours, these colors obtained from organic raw materials faded, evaporated, and Callas emerged as something lifeless, like a mummy. I knew that this signified death. Pier Paolo was very affectionate with Callas, but only affectionate. He wanted to distance himself from her to avoid hurting her. The film was nearing its end and he also wanted to cut the sentimental ties born during his artistic endeavor.

"As far as he was concerned, the relationship with Callas was over. But at precisely this time something happened that made Callas believe that Pier Paolo was also in love with her. I was the involuntary cause of the equivocation. The film was finished and Pier Paolo said to me: 'We should give Maria a present. Think of something suitable that will help her remember these times in Friuli.' I had no idea what to give to such a woman as Callas. Callas had

everything. Then, remembering that we were staying near Aquileia, a famous Roman city with extraordinary artistic relics, I decided to give her a ring with an inset of Aquileian corniola. Corniola is a hard stone, dating from ancient Roman times, carved with tiny engravings; it is not only of great artistic worth but also has a magical, esoteric meaning. I found a fine example, took it to a famous goldsmith in Udine and had it mounted like ancient rings. Pier Paolo

liked it very much. We organized a huge party, at my home, and invited one hundred fifty people. It was July and we ate outside, on the large lawn in front of the house. Maria was very happy. At a certain point, Pier Paolo asked me for the ring and gave it to Callas. She was taken aback and didn't know what to say. They kissed.

"For Maria, the ring and the kiss were the definitive proof of Pasolini's love for her. For him, on the other hand,

they were the token of a task brought to a happy conclusion. After the party, he began to lose interest in Callas, while she was all eyes for him. After about a fortnight, the telephone rang at half past six in the morning, while I was in my studio. It was Maria. She was crying desperately. 'When is he going to make

"I was amazed. I would never have dreamed such a thing. I tried to calm her down. I promised to speak to Pasolini. I phoned him in his hotel. 'It's very important,' I said to him, 'It's about Maria, I have to see you. I'll pick you up in half an hour.'

"When I arived, Pier Paolo was waiting for me at the main door of the hotel. He got into my car and as we drove I told him about Maria's telephone call. 'You have to talk to her,' I said. He remained silent for a long time. He wasn't surprised, shocked, or pained. He rather seemed as if he had expected this reaction from Maria. He went to see her. They spoke together at length. I have no idea what they said to each other. He did not like to talk about his sexual preferences. He lived his

A student asked her: 'What is the best way to interpret a piece of music?' 'Love it,' she answered.

his mind up?' she asked me. 'He even gave me an engagement ring. When will he decide to marry me? I can't carry on like this, I can't stand it any more, I feel I'm going to die.' I listened, aghast. I couldn't utter a single word. Maria went on: 'You are his best friend, please tell him, tell him to make up his mind, I can't stand all this waiting.'

homosexuality as a kind of trauma. However, he managed to sort out the situation calmly and serenely. Maria and Pier Paolo were to remain good friends. He later dedicated several poems to her, one of which is entitled 'The Ring.'"

She realized she had humiliated herself but was neither angry with herself nor with Pasolini. On the contrary,

Opposite page, left:

Maria Callas with friends and actors on the set of Pier Paolo Pasolini's Medea. Callas was greatly struck by the director, to the point of falling in love

with him, even thinking they could get married.

Opposite page, right:

1969. Pasolini on the island of Safon, in the lagoon around Grado, explaining certain scenes of the film Medea to Callas.

Side: Maria Callas on the set of Medea, being filmed by Pasolini (kneeling at the camera).

Above:

1970. Maria Callas in Paris with Pier Paolo Pasolini for the premiere of Medea. Unfortunately, the film was not as popular with audiences as Callas had hoped.

in comparison with her experience with Onassis, she found the whole episode rather pure and innocent. And, as the many letters she later wrote to Pasolini clearly show, in her heart she developed a maternal affection for the poet. In these letters, full of wisdom, advice, and suggestions, Maria confided her convictions to Pasolini, her belief in God, and consoled him over the sentimental difficulties he was experiencing at the time. She wrote: "I'm not your mother, my dear," but in truth what she wrote and the tone she used were typical of a sweet and tender mother.

Maria was very brave in overcoming this embarrassing situation but, in reality, she once again had to mark up a defeat, taste the bitterness of yet another disappointment.

Another disappointment. Destiny persecuted her. Above all, the film did not bring her the satisfaction and prestige she craved. Undoubtedly, it has a certain artistic value and remains the work of a great film director whose search into the myth of Medea achieves certain touching moments. But it was

generally ignored by the public at large. And Maria, to emerge from the ditch that Onassis had thrown her into, needed the support of the masses. The experiment thus proved to be a fiasco. But she didn't complain even about this. She had become wiser. At the time, she confided to writer Dacia Maraini, who she had met through Pasolini: "Callas is sweet and does not have claws. She does her duty, works, and is never satisfied with what she does. But everyone says she is aloof, but this is untrue. They judge me without knowing me. I am too proud to defend myself and I let them say what they want. But then I am upset about all the false things they say about me, passing me off as an avaricious and ambitious woman."

Having finished her commitments with the film, the desperation of ordinary life returned. Maria had to find another distraction, and this time she turned to music. She accepted the offer to hold a finishing course for young singers at the Juilliard School in New York.

She also decided to resume exercising her own voice, with the secret hope of singing in theaters once again. She wrote to François Valery, her Parisian friend: "Just think, here I am writing to you! I am very busy, you know. I'm studying. . . I began yesterday, whether you believe me or not. . . I really hope

you will write me a few lines every now and then because I can't return before mid-November. I shall insist on studying all month, then the course will start. With great affection, Maria."

The special course began on October 11, 1971. It was held onstage at the Juilliard Theater and was attended

corner and buy an ice cream?' We left the hotel, walked around the block and bought an ice cream on the street. It was an expedient to delay the moment when she would be left alone with her own company."

Those attending the course at the Juilliard School discovered that her

"Callas is sweet and does not have claws. She does her duty, works, and is never satisfied with what she does. But everyone says she is aloof, but this is untrue. They judge me without knowing me. I am too proud to defend myself and I let them say what they want. But then I am upset about all the false things they say about me, passing me off as an avaricious and ambitious woman."

by crowds of people. As well as young singers, there were also famous artists, such as Zeffirelli, Placido Domingo, Tito Gobbi, and Grace Bumbry.

One evening, Tito Gobbi invited her to dinner, together with his wife and her daughter Cecilia. "At the end of the dinner," the famous baritone related, "I accompanied her back to the Plaza. Before taking the lift, she turned to me and said: 'You know, Tito, I'm alone, I'm really alone here. . . I don't even have a little dog. Why don't we pop round the

lessons were flat and even somewhat boring. This is evident from listening to them and reading them in the book and CD. Callas communicated no technical secrets or magical formulas about how to become a great stage performer. She said rather obvious things. Yet, perhaps, in the final analysis, precisely these are the most important things. She coldly asked a young tenor who had interpreted the duet from the first act of *Madam Butterfly*: "Do you or do you not know what you are saying?" He replied: "Of course. I'm saying: 'Now you are all mine.'" She retorted, "Then sing what you are saying."

To a soprano who had just finished singing "Caro nome" from *Rigoletto*, she said: "You see, Gilda is a girl full of passion. You must communicate this feeling of palpitating emotion to the audience even before you begin singing. Breathing itself is an emotional expression."

To a tenor who was lacking in intensity: "Come on, put more passion

In the spring of 1972, the course at the Juilliard School was coming to an end and Maria was sad. She had to return to the solitude that was devouring her and she sought some other opportunity to grasp so that she wouldn't succumb. She was tormented by insomnia and phoned friends at unthinkable hours. Maestro Eugene Khon, who was her pianist at the Juilliard School, recalls that Maria phoned him in the middle of the night: "Perhaps you were asleep?" she asked

"This evening I'm singing my fifth concert. Thank God.

I am happy, dear Leo. The public cares for me.

Naturally, they know my voice isn't what it was fifteen years ago.

But they are so happy! Why then should I complain?

Working hard has always been good for me."

into it. You are from Naples, so you have no excuse." And when he moved to embrace Callas, she said: "No, no gestures, you must express yourself only with your voice."

A Korean baritone sang the prologue to *Pagliacci*: "You have a voice, bring it out. I'm not bothered if you break the sharp, what matters is that you give it some power."

A student asked her: "What is the best way to interpret a piece of music?" "Love it," she answered.

timidly. "No, no," he replied and they began talking, talking about anything. The important thing was to pass time and not to be alone. It was at this time that her relationship with Giuseppe Di Stefano began. They had sung together in wonderful operas at La Scala and around the world. "When I heard her sing for the first time, in Mexico in 1952," he told us, "I was astonished and said to myself 'She sings like a man.'" It was Callas who wanted Di Stefano with her at La Scala a few months later because she had recognized his exceptional artistic talent with which, on stage, she felt in perfect harmony. Together, they formed a legendary artistic pairing, giving life to unforgettable events. But they both had strong characters and for this reason often argued. Now, destiny brought them together again. Maria was going through a dreadful period and Di Stefano, an artist, unconventional, ironic, and a Casanova, but nevertheless sensitive and very humane, came to her aid.

Di Stefano played an extremely important role in this period of Maria Callas's life. A great deal has been written about what happened between 1972 and 1975. Many have accused the great tenor of having exploited Callas, making her sing even when her voice had gone, only for money. Di Stefano, despite appearances, is a shy and reserved man

and has never wanted to discuss the matter. Demonstrating immense personal dignity, he has preferred to suffer vulgar accusations rather than reveal the secrets of his private life with Callas. Yet so much time has gone by and news has become history. On one occasion when we met the tenor, he revealed his own version of events. "Callas came back to life with me," he opened. "She came out of the tunnel of despair and rediscovered the certainties and joys of past times. She laughed and joked. She could also be capricious, as she was when we were at La Scala together. The atmosphere of concerts, the rustle of applause from 'her' audience, which had never forgotten her, were like a miraculous medicine.

"In 1972, I was passing through New York. The year before I had given performances in Japan and Korea and the organizers of that tour asked me to come back with a soprano. They made

Opposite page:

1980. Giovan Battista Meneghini, in a photo taken just before his death. Meneghini always kept an eye from a distance on his wife's affairs, without ever attempting to make up with her. He wouldn't give her a divorce because he didn't want her to marry again.

Center:

1970. Maria Callas with Pier Paolo Pasolini at the premiere of the film Medea in Paris.

Below:

1969. Maria Callas with Pier Paolo Pasolini on the set of Medea. Pasolini was enthusiastic about Callas

and on one occasion declared: "We are in the presence of an artist who, in a certain sense, is the most modern of women. However, an ancient creature lives inside her, strange, mysterious, arcane, hiding terrible interior conflicts. I am perfectly aware of her professional skills but they matter little to me. It was her human individuality that convinced me Callas could be my Medea."

me three offers: 4,000 dollars for Anna Moffo, 6,000 dollars for Renata Tebaldi and 10,000 dollars for Maria Callas. I phoned Moffo and Tebaldi to inform them, but neither bothered to reply.

"I didn't even phone Callas because I thought she was no longer interested in giving concerts.

"In New York, having lunch with a friend, I mentioned the offer from Japan. He said: 'Let's phone Callas straight-away, she's here in New York.' 'Forget it,' I said, but he phoned immediately. Maria was not in her hotel room, so he left a message saying I was looking for her. As we left the restaurant, I stopped at a florist and sent Callas some flowers.

"In the evening, I was at the home of actor Ben Gazzara who had organized a party in my honor. The phone rang and Ben answered; I heard him say: 'I'll send him to you immediately.' He looked at me and said: 'It's Maria Callas. She says she's been looking for you

everywhere. She wants to see you. Get going.' 'But, Ben, you're having a party for me.' He simply said: 'It doesn't matter, Maria is more important.'

"I went to the hotel and up to her room. It was almost midnight. I knocked at Maria's door. She opened it and said: 'I know, you have always cared about me.' I said: 'I suppose this means I can come in?' And she never let me go again. Maria was destroyed, completely down in the dumps. She kept on saying: 'Every day that passes is a day less for me to live.' 'You must sing again,' I told her. 'My voice has gone,' she said. 'It'll come back if you sing,' I insisted. The day after we went to the pianist with whom she studied every now and then. Maria went up to the piano trembling like a leaf. She began singing but didn't have a note in her voice. I embraced her and said: 'Let's go, let's go for a walk in Central Park.' She was crying and was terribly frightened. 'I realized that only singing could renew her will to live and I kept on telling her that she should overcome her fears and get back in touch with the theater.

"Maria began studying with me. At the time, she couldn't put two notes together. She had no wind, she'd forgotten how to breathe properly, how to control her diaphragm. She despaired at times, shouting and crying with anger: 'I'll never be able to do it.' 'I'll get you back in shape,' I said repeatedly. She

Korea. Audiences were numerous and applauded ecstatically, especially in Paris, London, New York, and Germany, where Callas had fanatical admirers. Every theater was sold out even if the tickets were rather expensive. The critics were ferocious: Every one of them was against her, cold, cynical, and malicious. "The 'divine Callas' sings as if she had a dentist's drill in her mouth," wrote Figaro after the concert in Paris. Maria, however, was happy and didn't

for a long time, we were the protagonists of romantic stories onstage all over the world, forming an envied, unique couple. Later, when we met again in 1972, true passion reared its head. We were very much in love. We understood each other perfectly, which meant, at the same time, that we could be free. We were not only passionate, there was something more: infinite tenderness, artistic complicity of the highest level, the desire to win again, mature love."

That concert tour was truly revitalizing for Callas, although she was worried at the outset. Towards the end of September 1973, she wrote to her godfather and major confidant, Dr. Leonidas Lantzounis: "I am preparing a concert tour and I'm scared stiff but I hope to stay well and be calm enough for the first concert, scheduled for the 22nd of

"My voice, you are right, is making enormous progress. Just think, if I'd not had my dreadful stomach! My voice is so much more focused and firm! I'm on the right road at last, Jesus! I'm getting used to the good old sounds. I can't believe it. . ."

had to start all over from scratch, just like a beginner. But she made a tremendous effort with utterly moving enthusiasm. In a few months, I helped her get back in form and we began to sing together again.

"In three years, we completed a world tour of around fifty concerts. We went from one city to another, one country to the next, living in luxury hotels, as in the good old times."

The long concert tour began in Hamburg on October 25, 1973, and ended two years later on October 29, 1975. Maria and Di Stefano performed in all the major cities of Europe and the United States and ended in Japan and

read the newspapers.

"In 1973, the Nuovo Teatro Regio in Turin was to be inaugurated with Verdi's *I Vespri Siciliani* and the management asked Callas to direct the opera," Di Stefano went on. "Maria answered: 'I will only accept if I can work with Pippo Di Stefano.' She never wanted to stay away from me. And, by being together so much, we fell in love. It could hardly have been different. Since our first meeting in 1952, we'd known we were made for each other. It was love at first sight, artistically speaking of course. We were both married and didn't have the slightest thought of ruining our lives with an illicit relationship. So,

this month, because expectations are enormous and I am logically not the same as I was when I was thirty-five. Let's hope everything turns out for the best." In November, she wrote from Frankfurt: "This evening I'm singing my fifth concert. Thank God. I am happy, dear Leo. The public cares for me. Naturally, they know my voice isn't what it was fifteen years ago. But they are so happy! Why then should I complain? Working hard has always been good for me."

She didn't even hide her relationship with Di Stefano from her godfather, although she wrote with a certain detachment and irony, demonstrating that she felt she was navigating in troubled waters. "I am still with Pippo. I haven't found anyone better. Richer, perhaps, but poorer in sentiment. All

this, naturally, contradicts my inclinations. We should have fallen in love when he was famous (and had a stupendous voice) because he has many human qualities."

She went on: "I am still very fond of Pippo but obviously not as much as before. Yet how can I tell him? After the death of his daughter, he lives only because of our love. I want to hope that destiny will work things out for the best, so that the shock won't be too much for him. He's not the kind of man to fall in love with another woman. I hope it for him but I doubt it.

"I could meet someone. It would be the ideal solution. In such an event, it wouldn't matter to me if he suffered or not (that's a horrible thing to say, isn't it?)."

The relationship, as Callas makes

quite clear in these letters, began to go through difficult times. "Maria and I are too similar," Di Stefano told us. "I am a hot-blooded Sicilian with a strong sense of dignity and independence. Maria was Greek, the old-fashioned kind. When she was in love, she was possessive, invasive, and jealous. She was ferociously, blindly jealous. She was worse than Othello, and I believe she would have been able to kill out of jealousy.

"I was then in a delicate situation. I was married and she was jealous of my wife. At that time, my relationship with my wife was merely formal. We stayed together simply because our family was going through a terrible drama: My daughter, Luisa, nineteen, had a tumor. Maria was very close to me during this tragedy but couldn't wait. She should have understood that it was not the right time to think of divisions, separations, divorce, and the like. We needed to wait for time to heal these tremendous

wounds and for things to work out on their own. But, as I said, she was jealous, blind, and acted impulsively just like a child, making awful mistakes which I could neither accept nor pretend not to see. She ruined everything in this way. At a certain moment, we began to argue seriously; our wonderful understanding became strained and finally snapped. At the end of the long tour, we each went our own way."

Nevertheless, it had been a special experience, particularly from an artistic point of view. Giuseppe Di Stefano had promised Callas that, by singing, in two years she would have overcome all the technical difficulties which prevented her from achieving the same heights as she had in the past. It was the right way ahead. Callas also realized this. She wrote one night to Di Stefano: "Pippetto,

I couldn't sleep tonight and so I mustered up the courage to listen to the concert on the 8th (the concert held in Paris on December 8, 1973). I was amazed. My voice, as you said, is making enormous progress. Just think, if I'd not had my dreadful stomach! My voice is so much more focused and firm! I'm on the right road at last, Jesus!!! I'm getting used to the good old sounds. I can't believe it. Thank God we have these tapes. . ."

There is a recording of the last concert, in Seoul, Korea, given on October 29, 1975. Maria is superb and her voice is fresh. She sang some airs from *Carmen* with Pippo in French. But after that concert, the nightmare of solitude

157

Opposite page, left:

1973. Maria Callas with Giuseppe Di Stefano in London. Having sung famous operas together on the stages of half the world, the Sicilian tenor and the Greek soprano met again in 1972 and their love story lasted until 1975.

Opposite page, right:

1973. Another snapshot of Callas and Di Stefano. Callas had given up singing some years beforehand but Di Stefano convinced her to resume her career and they sang in a tour that embraced the whole world.

Left:

1974. Maria Callas and Giuseppe Di Stefano in Japan as members of the jury for the Madam Butterfly Award. With them, left, is soprano Wilma Vernocchi, who took first prize that year.

Above:

1973. Maria Callas, at the end of a concert performed with Di Stefano in Paris, receives flowers from an admirer.

returned to Callas. She returned to Paris, while Di Stefano went to Australia for a tour on his own. "Callas kept on trying to contact me," Di Stefano said. "When I returned to Italy, there were many messages. I went immediately to Paris, but I was unable to see her. The people around her told me on the phone that she was unwell and could not see anyone. I knew they were lying but I could hardly break down the door to the apartment to see her. I had rushed to her immediately, proving what I felt for her. But I couldn't do anything else."

Maria went into a slow and mysterious decline. Her loneliness became even more unbearable following the death of people who, for better or worse, had played an important role in her life and to whom she was still very attached. Aristotle Onassis died on March 15, 1975, having suffered for several months from serious miasthenia, an illness of the neuro-muscular system. Two days later, Luchino Visconti also died; following a stroke, he had been confined to a wheelchair for twelve months. At dawn on November 2, 1975, Pier Paolo Pasolini was found killed in a desolate, sandy spot in Fiumicino, near Rome.

Despite everything that had happened between them, Onassis always remained an important person for her. "When Maria and I were together," Di Stefano told us, "Onassis telephoned almost every evening. Maria went into the adjacent room and they talked for hours in Greek. To a certain extent, Maria still depended on Onassis and his staff. His secretaries renewed her passport, made hotel bookings, arranged flights, renewed her credit cards, organized all her bureaucratic requirements."

The death of these friends depressed her immensely. Show business had forgotten her, put her firmly to one side. The jet set now ignored her completely; friends, even the most faithful, were all busy with their own business. After Maria's death, many regretted not having understood her dramatic situation and not having done more to help her. The only people who kept her company were her two servants, Bruna and Ferruccio. Callas spent the evenings playing cards with them and when it came to their day off, she begged them with tears in her eyes to stay at home and not leave her alone.

The last two years of the soprano's life are shrouded in mystery. There is a document that could throw some light on the period and answer many questions, but it is locked away in secret. It is a kind of diary, around 150 letter-headed pages with Callas's Paris address printed in the top right corner. Maria dashed down her thoughts on these sheets of paper, in French, noting her impressions, feelings, state of mind, and events which concerned her. On her death, this diary came into the possession of a friend of Callas, the lawyer who administered her business affairs. "As long as I live, this diary will never be published," the lawyer proclaimed. Subsequently, these pages changed hands several times and are currently owned by an Italian doctor, Ivano Signorini, who, having read them, in turn decided to keep them secret. Why? What surprises can they hold in store?

It is difficult to formulate an answer. The present owner of this diary, with whom we have been in touch, is a great admirer of Maria Callas and a person of considerable moral standing. He believes that the contents of the diary have nothing to add to the art of the "Divine Callas" but would only exacerbate the gossip and mystery surrounding the death of the soprano. Out of sincere pity and respect, he has decided not to make the diary public. In our duty as journalists, we can say that this diary could well reveal another sad chapter in the life of Maria Callas, reveal yet another drama. We have been able to read photocopies of some of these sheets of paper. They contain messages of terrible despair. Short, concise, desolate sentences, jotted down in firm handwriting, with just one or two comments on each page, almost like messages, like a cry for help in the wilderness. "I know of no affection or esteem for me: I am infinitely alone." "Callas: but Maria?" "I have never depended on anyone in my life: Today I am the slave to a bottle of pills." At times, Maria makes strange references to drugs: "I think that, for me, ending this life will be a joy: I have no happiness, no friends, only drugs." At times she complains because the person who should bring her "these drugs" is late. Every note is despondently signed "Maria."

It is impossible to say what worth these remarks may have. It would be necessary to read them all. The fact remains, however, that in the last years of her life, Callas experienced serious problems through her use of psycho-pharmaceuticals, sedatives, and stimulants.

"She suffered tremendously from insomnia, even when she was young," Di Stefano told us. "Many of her letters begin, 'It's 6:00 in the morning and I haven't slept a wink all night.' I've been told that when she was with Onassis, he behaved so badly at times that he took occasional girlfriends onboard the *Christina* for orgies. Maria, despairing and sickened, closed herself in her cabin and took sleeping pills so that she wouldn't hear the outrageous laughter of the party. It was then that she began using strong drugs, which deadened her, sent her into a state of utter drowsiness. In the morning, however, she had to take equally strong stimulants to wake up.

"Sleeping pills were her ruin, We were dining one evening in her apartment. She suddenly got up and went to take the pills and came back not wearing anything. She had already taken some pills but had then forgetton whether she had taken them or not and took them again, reducing herself to a state of total idiocy.

"On another occasion, in a hotel in Hamburg, I couldn't find her anywhere. I went to her room but she wasn't there. Worried, I called the maids. We searched everywhere and finally found her: She had fallen off the other side of the bed and was sleeping on the floor, dead to the world because of the pills she had taken."

The question arises whether, in the last years of her life, she mixed the sleeping pills she had been taking for years with other drugs which proved fatal for her heart.

Maria Callas died on September 16, 1977. Her servants explained that Maria got up late, around noon, had breakfast in bed, and then stumbled to the bathroom. She had told her housekeeper Bruna that she had a bad pain in her left arm. "This year, my rheumatism has

begun to trouble me earlier than usual," she had said. She complained about the strange pain in her arm that morning as well.

Soon after she went to the bathroom, the servants heard a thud. They ran to the bathroom and found Maria on the floor. They called the doctor but he was out. They phoned the American Hospital but the number was busy. They finally called faithful Ferruccio's doctor, who came immediately and could only confirm that Maria Callas was dead. In the death certificate, he simply wrote "heart attack."

The death of Maria Callas may therefore have been caused by a heart attack but, in truth, nothing precise was ever revealed. No autopsy was performed. The funeral was held in the Orthodox Church on Tuesday September 19, but in the three days between her death and the funeral, nobody, not even friends, was allowed to view her corpse. After the religious ceremony, her coffin was taken to the cemetery and, from there, immediately sent for cremation. The people who organized the funeral said that Callas had written in her will that she wanted to be cremated. But the will was never found. It is common practice for cremations to take place the day after the arrival of the deceased; moreover, French law requires that it must be requested by a member of the family. This requirement was not observed in Maria's case. The register of Père Lachaise Cemetery records the request for cremation signed by Jean Roer, who was merely the administrator of Maria's business affairs.

Opposite page:

1975. Maria Callas and Giuseppe Di Stefano during one of their performances on the concert tour in Japan.

Side:

1972. Maria Callas and Giuseppe Di Stefano in Milan, in the early days of their love story. Callas wanted Di Stefano to leave his wife so that she could marry the tenor but he refused to do so because, at the time, his daughter was seriously ill with cancer.

Above:

1975. Maria Callas and Giuseppe Di Stefano in Tokyo during their tour of Japan.

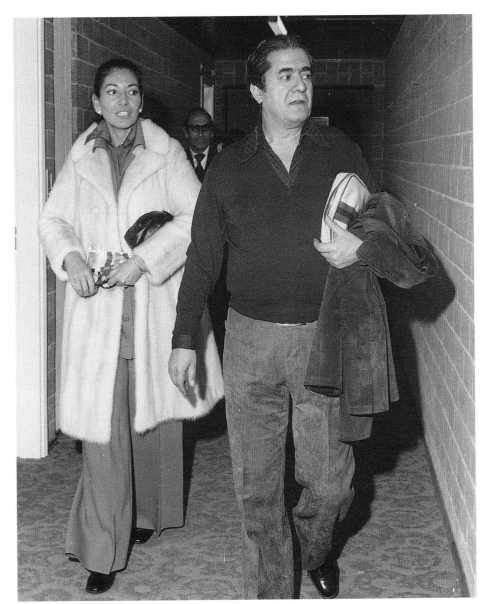

days before she died: "I really miss Sirmione." She added: "I have done many good things in my life but I have also made many mistakes and now I am paying for them."

She was thinking about Meneghini and even this curious note seems to confirm the idea. It was written on a piece of blue letter-headed paper from the Savoy Hotel in London. In the top right corner, there is the date—summer 1977—indicating that it was written at this time or at most only a few weeks before her death. Underneath the date, there are the letters "A T." Which can only mean "A Titta" (for Titta). Maria, as

me. My heart tempts me. The last voice of my destiny, the last cross of my life). They are verses from Ponchielli's *Gioconda*, which the protagonist sings in Act Three. Maria, in writing them down, missed the single word of the first line: "Suicidio" (Suicide).

Why did Maria write this note? Why did she leave out the word "suicide"? What did she mean by it all?

Meneghini maintained that his wife had committed suicide and that the note proved it. Giuseppe Di Stefano thinks that Maria's heart, strained by sleeping pills and stimulants, finally stopped beating. Whatever the truth is, the caus-

The ashes of Maria Callas were placed in a small loculus in the basement of the cemetery. The loculus was marked N. 16258. Many people went there to pray and place flowers but after eighteen months it emerged that the loculus was empty: The ashes had been removed and placed in a bank vault. In 1980, again saying that everything was in accordance with Maria's wishes, the ashes were thrown into the Aegean Sea during an evocative but rather rhetorical ceremony. Nothing now remains of Maria Callas. Should anyone ever have wanted to investigate the real causes of her death, it would have been impossible to examine anything, not even the handful of ashes left after cremation.

The doubt that her death was not caused entirely by natural causes emerges from a note Callas wrote, found in a prayer book on her bedside table. It is a strange and mysterious note and, what is more, is addressed to her husband, Meneghini, who she had left in 1959 for Onassis.

Towards the end of her life, Maria realized all the mistakes she had made. Her disappointments helped her understand that, probably, the most sincere man she had ever met in her life was Meneghini. She may even have hoped for a reconciliation. This is clear from certain details. For example, when a German journalist asked when she intended to write her memoirs, she answered: "There is only one person who could write them because he knows everything about me: my husband." She confided to a friend a few

we have seen in her letters, often used this short name for her husband. There are five lines underneath: *In questi fieri momenti, tu sol mi resti. E il cor mi tenti. L'ultima voce del mio destino, ultima croce del mio cammin* (In these proud moments, only you are left for

es of her death are shrouded in mystery.

Mystery in death and a mystery over her will. Maria was very rich. During her career, she had been one of the most highly paid singers in the history of opera and had managed her money very shrewdly. After her death, where did Callas's fortune end up?

Maria had no children and was separated from Meneghini, but not divorced. Immediately after her death, the newspapers continued talking about a mysterious last will and testament and there were considerable expectations to learn who would inherit her fortune. Somebody recalled that, when she had gone to Milan to sing at the Instituto del Tumori, she was so struck by her meeting with the patients there, especially the young people such as Di Stefano's daughter, that she said: "When I die, I want to leave all my money to this Institute." Yet the days and weeks went

by without any trace of a will.

Meneghini was equally curious to find out the contents of her will and telephoned Paris occasionally for any news. One night, about a month after Maria's death, as he himself narrated, he had a dream about her in which she said: "Titta, remember the will." She repeated this three times.

Meneghini couldn't understand the meaning of these words. He kept on thinking about them, but had no explanation. He dreamed about his wife again the following night and she repeated the same words: "Titta, remember the will." In the morning, ruminating over this

Opposite page, left:

1970. Maria Callas complimenting Renata Scotto, who had taken her place at La Scala in Milan.

Opposite page, right:

A portrait of Maria Callas by Piacenza-born painter Ulisse Sartini. The painting is now in the New Music Theater, Athens.

161

Side:

1965. Maria Callas in a scene from Tosca, performed in February at the Paris Opera and directed by Franco Zeffirelli. It was one of her last stage appearances and a major triumph.

Above:

1975 . Maria Callas during the tour with Di Stefano in Japan. Sitting next to the tenor is his wife, Maria.

strange dream, he remembered something that happened in 1954. He and his wife were about to leave for America and had gone to the offices of their lawyer, Professor Trabucchi, in Verona, to leave him certain instructions. The lawyer, when he learned they were leaving for America, said: "You travel continuously, have you never thought about making wills on behalf of each other? I certainly hope nothing will happen to you but if something dreadful were ever to happen then at least there would be fewer worries for whoever survived." "You are quite right," said Maria. "We have never thought about it, but it would be a good idea to arrange everything immediately." "In the meantime," said the lawyer, "write your intentions here in my diary." On one page, Maria wrote: "In the event of my death, I leave everything to my husband, Giovan Battista Meneghini." On another page, Meneghini expressed the same desire on behalf of his wife. Meneghini suddenly remembered this fact, but how could the document be traced? Professor Trabucchi had died some years previously. He had six assistants in his studio but they had gone their own ways after his death. Where could the diary be?

He tried to remember the names of the lawyers who worked with Professor Trabucchi. One immediately came to mind and he found the telephone number. It was Sunday morning but he called nonetheless and managed to speak with the lawyer. He told him about the dreams and the will and asked if it would be possible to trace the diary. "Who knows where it has ended up?" the lawyer said. "However, I have some

Opposite page:

1976. Maria Callas in the streets of Paris in one of the last photographs taken of her. The note adjacent has the words she wrote a few weeks before her death. They are taken from Ponchielli's opera Gioconda. This note led many to believe that she thought about, and finally enacted, taking her own life.

Side:

Maria Callas outside her house in Via Buonarrotti, Milan.

papers, from the time I worked with Trabucchi, in the attic, and one of these days I'll take a look at them."

A few minutes later, the phone rang in Meneghini's home. It was the lawyer: "I've been up to my attic," he said, "and found a file with the diary in it. I've found Maria's will."

Meneghini took the papers to Paris. He gave them to the judge who confirmed their authenticity. Since, within the period defined by law, no other last

with a signed document, a few lines written shortly before his death in which Meneghini named his housekeeper as his sole heir. Emma Brutti was seventy-eight and had looked after him for twenty years. The entire wealth of the businessman and everything he had inherited from Maria Callas, as well as the royalties due from records sold in years to come, went to the family of an ordinary old woman whose only merit was having been a diligent and respect-

"I know of no affection or esteem for me: I am infinitely alone. I have never depended on anyone in my life: Today I am the slave to a bottle of pills. I think that, for me, ending this life will be a joy: I have no happiness, no friends, only drugs."

Above:

1970. A photo of Maria Callas smiling from the film Medea.

Pages 164-165:

Maria Callas in a dramatic interpretation of Donizetti's Poliuti, the opera in which the soprano inaugurated the 1960-1961 season at La Scala.

will and testament had been presented, the will presented by Meneghini was immediately approved and he inherited all Maria's wealth. Meneghini was already very rich on his own account. It is not known exactly what he inherited from Maria Callas, but it was undoubtedly a very significant sum of money.

Meneghini did not have any children and, moreover, he had argued with his family. After his death in January 1981, there was yet another huge surprise. His brothers, nephews, and nieces expected to inherit everything. But, out of the blue, the notary was presented

ful housekeeper. She, her children, and grandchildren, were to reap the benefit of all the money that Callas had earned through her incomparable art and the fortune that Meneghini had accumulated together through his business skills.

PHOTOGRAPHIC REFERENCES

The numbers refer to the pages; the abbreviations refer to the position of the photo on the page (top, bottom, center, right, left).
Archivio Editoriale Gli Olmi, Milan: 8l, 12r, 13l, 14, 16-18, 19b, 20-27, 28b, 29-31, 32t, 33l, 34 first and second from r, 36l, 38-41, 44-45, 47, 48b, 49b, 50-51, 52l, 53r, 55b, 56-61, 62r, 63-69, 71, 73, 74l, 74-75c, 76-77, 78r, 79, 80r, 81-92, 93r, 94-108, 109t and b, 110-113, 116-118, 119r, 120-125, 126b, 127l, 128-131, 132l, 133, 136-137, 138b, 139, 140l, 141-142, 143r, 144 second from l, 146, 147l, 148, 149r, 150l, 151r, 152t, 153, 154b, 155r, 156r, 157, 158b, 159r, 160, 161r, 162l, 163.
Archivio Tommasoli, Verona: 48-49t.
Centro Documentazione Mondadori, Segrate: 8r, 9, 12t, 13r, 15, 19t, 28t, 32b, 33t, 36r, 37, 42-43, 46l, 52c, 54l, 54-55t, 62l, 70, 72, 78l, 80l, 93l, 109r, 114-115, 119l, 126t, 127r, 131b, 132r, 134-135, 138t, 140r, 143l, 144l, 145r, 147r, 149t, 150r, 151l, 152l, 154-155t, 156b, 158r, 159l, 161l, 162r, 164-165.

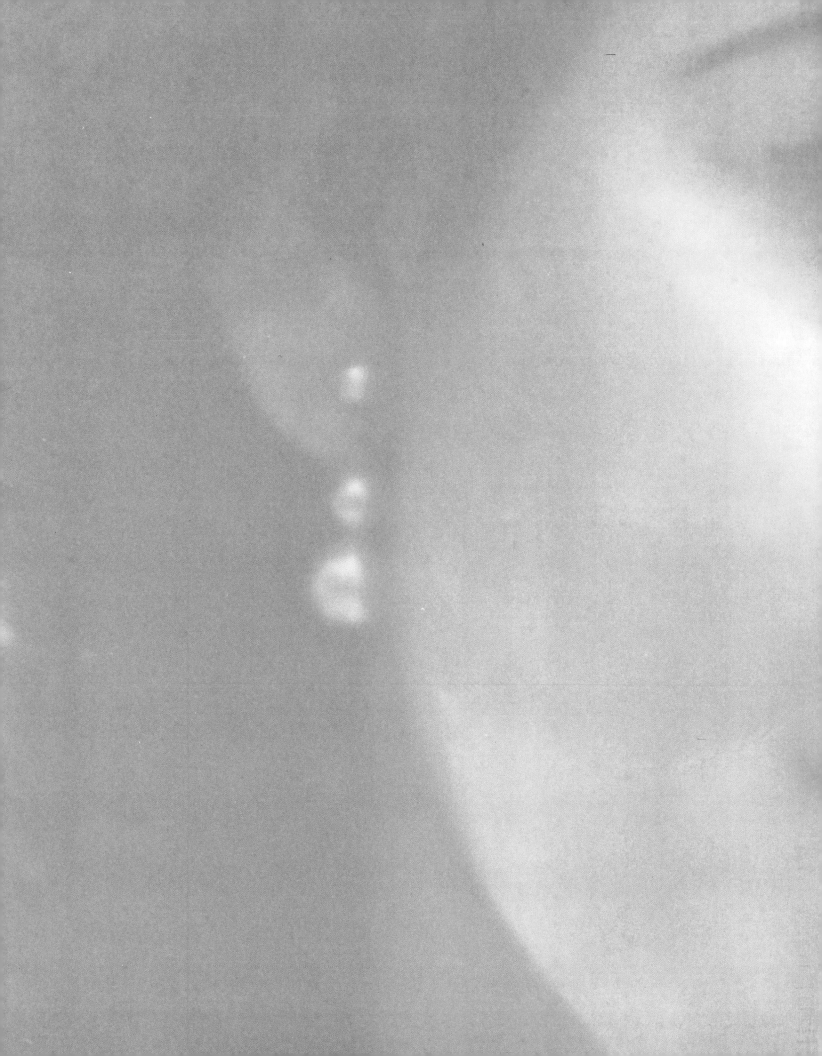